LONDON

WITH KIDS

AJ Sutherland

NEW HOLLAND

Published in 2015 by
New Holland Publishers
London • Sydney • Auckland

The Chandlery Unit 009 50 Westminster Bridge Road London SE1 7QY United Kingdom
1/66 Gibbes Street Chatswood NSW 2067 Australia
5/39 Woodside Ave Northcote, Auckland 0627

www.newhollandpublishers.com

A record of this book is held at the British Library and the National Library of Australia.

ISBN: 9781742577166

Managing Director: Fiona Schultz
Publisher: Alan Whiticker
Project Editor: Holly Willsher
Cover Design: Andrew Quinlan
Design: Andrew Davies
Production Director: Olga Dementiev
Printer: Toppan Leefung Printing Ltd (China)

10 9 8 7 6 5 4 3 2 1

Follow New Holland Publishers on
Facebook: www.facebook.com/NewHollandPublishers

Contents

Introduction

London is a simply wonderful city. Steeped in history, it is an exciting blend of legendary stories, cutting-edge architecture, exquisite green spaces and vibrant culture.

I've been lucky enough to experience London on many levels – as a resident and a tourist, with and without children. And though life in London as an aspiring twenty-something journalist was very different to now seeing London through my children's eyes, my love for this magical city never tires.

After travelling the world with my kids, every time I come back to London, I'm always amazed at the commitment the city has to making life easy for visiting families. Kids activities and interests are interwoven into many of the attractions and entertainment spaces, making them appealing to adults and children alike.

Even as a bustling commercial hub, home to over 8 million people and over 30 million tourists every year, London seems to do it effortlessly and do it well – with a little slice of that quintessentially understated British charm thrown in for good measure.

So, though you might not be able to sample London's sensational nightlife and fine dining now that you are visiting with kids, it is possible for the whole family to still enjoy the many things this magnificent city has to offer… before heading home for a glass of milk and an early night.

Unfortunately, to include every available kid-friendly attraction and restaurant in London is an impossible task, and any omissions do not mean that those places are *not* child-friendly. Instead, I have endeavoured to include a bit of everything, including some special ones off the beaten track – those that are nice and easy to visit with small children or are of particular interest to kids whilst still being interesting for adults. Places that kids will get something out of; that show something unique to London – its history, culture – without being excruciatingly patronising for parents.

My whole family always has a wonderful time exploring London and I hope that you can use this book as a starting point to find your own adventures.

Can we go in there?

The best of London's child-friendly attractions

Visitors to London are spoilt for choice, with things to do that suit every age and every budget. Nowadays, many attractions go out of their way to appeal to both kids and adults, so with a bit of planning everyone can enjoy the best that London has to offer.

KEY:
£££approx = £1–£10 per adult
£££approx = £11–20 per adult
£££approx = £21–30 per adult
££££ = £31+ per adult

Battersea Park Children's Zoo

Battersea Park, Battersea, London, SW11 4NJ

WEB:	www.batterseaparkzoo.co.uk
TEL:	+44 (0)20 7924 5826
EMAIL:	info@batterseaparkzoo.co.uk
COST:	£££request; children under 2 are free
OPENING TIMES:	10am–dusk
AGE RANGE:	3–10
BABY CARE:	heated mother and baby feeding room with baby change facilities
FOOD:	The Lemon Tree Café
NEAREST STATION:	Battersea Park (Overground line)

Battersea Children's Zoo is in the middle of Battersea Park, on the bank of the River Thames. Not a huge zoo, it is perfect for younger children to explore, with 41 different species of mammals, reptiles and birds, including monkeys, lemurs, snakes, chipmunks, meerkats, otters, emus, wallabies and parrots.

Battersea Zoo also has a farm area that has chickens, rabbits, pigs and a miniature Shetland pony, where kids can feed the animals (see website for feeding times) and learn about farming in England. Staff are really helpful and always nearby to answer the many animal-related questions that kids tend to have, and everything is clearly signposted with good descriptions on all of the enclosures.

The zoo has a lovely adventure play area, with a tractor to 'drive', a real life fire engine to sit in, plenty of play equipment for younger and older kids, a sandpit, a trampoline, as well as a chalkboard barn for any artists in the family. The combination of play equipment and animals, as well as the reasonable entry price, makes Battersea Zoo a really workable family day out.

There is plenty of seating across the site and lots of space for a picnic. There is also a pleasant café for lunch with a good children's menu.

The zoo is a 30-minute walk from the railway station, so take a pram for younger ones – the entire zoo is very pram-friendly. Otherwise, there are several buses from different areas of London that run past the park gate. With Battersea Park on the doorstep (see page 98 for more details), there is plenty to do once you leave the zoo as well.

Buckingham Palace

Buckingham Palace, London, SW1A 1AA

WEB:	www.royalcollection.org.uk
TEL:	+44 (0) 20 7766 7300
EMAIL:	bookinginfo@royalcollection.org.uk
COST:	£££; children under 5 are free
OPENING TIMES:	09.30am–6.30pm/7.30pm (closing times dependent on season)
AGE RANGE:	3+
BABY CARE:	change facilities available at the end of the visitor route
FOOD:	café at the end of the visitor route
NEAREST STATION:	Victoria (Victoria, District, Circle and overground lines), St James's Park (District and Circle lines), Hyde Park Corner (Piccadilly line)

No trip to London is complete without a visit to Buckingham Palace. You can wander past the entrance and simply take in the incredible architecture through the ornate gates, or you can pay to visit a number of different areas inside the Palace including the State Rooms, The Queen's Gallery, the Gardens and the Royal Mews.

Buckingham Palace is the working headquarters for the monarch. The Queen and the Duke of Edinburgh reside in private apartments at the Palace, and it is the London residence of several other members of the royal family. The Queen conducts the majority of her official duties from Buckingham Palace. Because it is a working royal residence, security is tight, so expect airport-style security at the entrance. Prams and bulky bags need to be checked in to the cloakroom and collected at the end of your visit (the Palace offers complimentary baby carriers for the duration of your tour).

There is a free audio tour that is well worth picking up, which gives plenty of facts and figures to help get the most out of your visit. Introduced by the Prince of Wales, it tells the history of Buckingham Palace and how it has evolved over the last 300 years. For the under 12s, there is a multimedia tour available that brings the palace history to life with the help of Rex the Corgi.

The 19 State Rooms, open for public viewing, are where the Queen receives and entertains visiting dignitaries. They are steeped in history and full of works of art, treasures from the Royal Collection and exquisite artefacts. One of the State Rooms includes the Picture Gallery, where some of the finest paintings from the Royal Collection are on display. The paintings are rotated frequently, with many from the collection on loan to exhibitions around the world. Other things to see include the Throne Room, the Ballroom – where Queen Victoria held lavish parties – and look out for the secret door that leads from the State Rooms to the Queen's private apartments.

There is also a Family Pavilion where kids can try out a traditional rocking horse, play giant puzzles and dress up in royal costumes (open during the summer months only). To help you find your way around the gardens, there is a free Garden Trail for kids, where you can see an abundance of wildlife (available to download from the website or collect in person at your visit).

A visit around Buckingham Palace usually takes about 2 hours. If you want to stay for tea, the Garden Café on the terrace that overlooks the Palace gardens, has a good selection of tea, cakes and drinks.

Separate to the State Rooms tour, the Queen's Gallery is an exhibition space, with rotating exhibitions on display (check website details). The gallery offers free family activity bags full of activities and puzzles for children to do as they explore the exhibition. There is also a family activity room, where children and adults can read books and see artefacts relevant to the current exhibition. There are interactive screens, costumes to dress up in, hats to wear, all of which change regularly to suit the exhibition on display.

Another separate tour is of the Royal Mews. An important branch of the Lord Chamberlain's office (which overseas significant business of the royal household) and one of the finest stables in the world, the Royal Mews provides transport for the royal family. Here you can see the various carriages and coaches used for royal occasions including weddings, coronations, and the State Opening of Parliament.

The Changing of the Guard can be seen every day outside the Palace and along Pall Mall. This colourful spectacle takes place at 11.00–11.30am every day in the summer, and alternate days in the winter (check website for up-to-date times). It can get busy outside the gates, and people begin to gather as early as 9.30am during school holidays, so to avoid the crowds head down Pall Mall instead to watch the Parade – it offers a much better vantage point for small people (and involves much less standing around time).

Cutty Sark

King William Walk, Greenwich, London, SE10 9HT

WEB:	www.rmg.co.uk/cuttysark
TEL:	+44 (0) 20 8312 6608
EMAIL:	cuttysarkbookings@rmg.co.uk
COST:	££££ (can be purchased as part of the Big Ticket, see page 172); children under 5 are free
OPENING TIMES:	10.00am–5.00pm (last admission 4.00pm)
AGE RANGE:	3+
BABY CARE:	change facilities available in accessible toilets on the ground floor; buggy park on the ground floor
FOOD:	café on the ground floor
NEAREST STATION:	Cutty Sark (DLR line), or catch the riverboat from Westminster to Greenwich Pier

Built in 1869, the *Cutty Sark* is a famous British clipper, which has sailed under both the British and Portuguese flag, visiting most major ports in the world. Well known as the fastest tea clipper, and one of the last to be built, she held the record sailing time from Britain to Australia for ten years. As steam technology grew, tea clippers were gradually replaced and in 1954 the *Cutty Sark* was placed in a permanent dry dock for public display.

Now a symbol of British maritime history this magnificent ship has become an iconic piece of London's waterfront landscape. After a fire in 2007, the ship underwent a meticulous restoration. Thankfully, more than 90 per cent of the original ship is still in place and the *Cutty Sark* is now one of London's leading tourist attractions.

The ship houses a museum, without a set path to follow – so it is nice to wander around and not feel rushed, and kids can take whatever detours they like, investigating all the nooks and crannies at their own pace.

You enter the ship at the cargo level, a space that is filled with artefacts, interactive displays and exhibits to bring to life the fascinating history of the ship. Here you can learn how and where the cargo was stored, see the original structure of the ship, and take part in a number of interactive displays – steering a course from Sydney to London, and experiencing life at sea in the 19th century.

On the main deck, visitors can walk through the cabins, see the bunk beds used by the sailors, explore the captains quarters, climb under the three masts which hold over 11 miles (17.7 km) of rigging, as well as taking in the expansive views of the river. The ship itself is now raised three metres (10 feet) from the ground, so once you are finished exploring the decks and holds of the ship, visitors can walk underneath the beautifully restored hull. There are a number of audio recordings for the kids to listen

to on telephones that retell stories of the sea, as well as the world's largest collection of figureheads – an impressive display in itself.

This lower level is also where you'll find the toilets, café and buggy park, and with plenty of benched seating around the perimeter, it is a good space for the kids to safely explore the exhibits and let off some steam.

The website has free museum trails to download which are well worth it for the younger kids; giving them things to tick off along the way. There is also an interactive app to download called Captain Woodget's Apprentice, which gives you important tasks to complete aboard the ship – ringing the bell, steering the ship, or even catching the mischievous monkeys that steal the Captain's sugar.

Located in Greenwich, the *Cutty Sark* is part of Royal Museums Greenwich (RMG), which includes the *Cutty Sark*, Royal Observatory (see page 38), National Maritime Museum (see page 74) and the Queen's House (see page 75). Tickets can be purchased as part of the Big Ticket, which gains you access to all paid attractions in the RMG group (see page 172).

Emirates Air Line and Aviation Experience

27 Western Gateway, London, E16 4FA;
Cable car runs between Greenwich Peninsula and the Royal Docks

WEB:	www.tfl.gov.uk/modes/emirates-air-line
	www.aviation-experience.com
TEL:	+44 (0)343 222 1234
COST:	£££; children under 5 are free
OPENING TIMES:	7.00am–9.00pm summer, 7.00am–8.00pm winter
AGE RANGE:	3+
NEAREST STATION:	Royal Victoria (DLR line), North Greenwich (Jubilee line)

Giving you a truly unique view of London, the Emirates Air Line is a cable car that operates from the Greenwich Peninsula (by the O2), across the Thames to the Royal Docks. You can get on at each end, and choose to travel one way or return.

The queues aren't usually long and the cable car journey doesn't take too much time – up to 10 minutes on a typical day – so it's a great little activity to do with kids who get antsy when stood for too long. The cars reach a height of 100 metres (295 feet) above the River Thames, and the views are fabulous – from Greenwich and along the Canary Wharf skyline.

You can travel on the cable car as part of the Emirates Air Line Experience ticket, or you can simply travel using an Oyster card (see page 168) for a much cheaper rate.

The Aviation Experience is a full package that includes a return trip on the cable car, an in-flight guide, and entrance into the Emirates Aviation Experience. The Aviation Experience is a new attraction that aims to provide an insight into modern air travel. There are interactive displays, life size aircraft models, and two commercial flight simulators that allow visitors to test their own take off and landing skills. The experience is split into zones: *Inflight*, where you can see what happens behind the scenes on a commercial A380 flight as well as explore the cockpit, *On the Ground* – a video wall and interactive game based on getting a plane ready for take-off, and the *Science of Flight* zone, which has a virtual wind tunnel and a scale model of a Rolls Royce Trent 800 engine made of LEGO®.

Because the cable car connects seamlessly with the underground network and is available on the Oyster card, many Londoners use the cable car as a daily mode of transport. You can take prams onto the cable car, but they must be folded flat and carried on the stairs that lead to the cable cars. The cable cars are closed in strong winds. Each carries 10 people.

HMS *Belfast*

The Queen's Walk, London, SE1 2JH

WEB:	www.iwm.org.uk/visits/hms-belfast
TEL:	+44 (0) 20 7940 6300
EMAIL:	hmsbelfast.iwm.org.uk
COST:	££££; children under 16 are free
OPENING TIMES:	10.00am–5.00pm/5.00pm daily (closing time dependent on season, check website for up-to-date information)
AGE RANGE:	4+
FOOD:	several cafes, all with child-friendly options
NEAREST STATION:	London Bridge (Northern and Jubilee lines)

HMS *Belfast* is a Royal Navy light cruiser that is now permanently moored in the River Thames and operated by the Imperial War Museum as a museum ship.

Launched in March 1938, *Belfast* played a significant role in the British naval campaigns during the Second World War, including supporting the Normandy landings. She was also operational in the Korean War from 1950–52. She was retired from active service in 1963, preserved as a museum ship in 1967, and opened to the public in 1971.

Aboard the huge ship, you can explore nine decks of naval life – almost all parts of the ship are open to the public. Clamber up ladders, along maze-like corridors, and discover what life was like on board as you wander through the dining rooms, living quarters, engine room, hospital and galleys. Exhibits cover every aspect of life at sea, from taking a shower to serving at war. Experience a battle engagement with the simulation of the Battle of North Cape, or run the ship in the interactive Operations Room. The main deck projects a film that recounts the ship's history, while special events and activities bring to life the ship's history in D-Day, the Arctic Convoys and the sinking of the *Scharnhorst*. The main deck is also where you'll find the Life at

Sea exhibition – a display of first-hand accounts from naval veterans, giving an insight into the life of sailors on board. From the main deck you'll have a unique view of Tower Bridge, and the city buildings along the Thames.

Grab a free audio guide on the way in – the extra information is excellent and will certainly add to the experience. Allow at least two hours to get all the way around, but you can easily spend much longer here.

HMS *Belfast* does not have cloakrooms or luggage areas and the corridors are small, so avoid taking any bulky bags along. Prams can go on '2' deck, but not on the rest of the ship. Also, the staircases are narrow and steep, so it is a museum best for those steady on their feet and who can navigate the steps. There is even a nice café on board near the visitor entrance for a drink and snack after all those ladders!

Hobbledown

Hobbledown Children's Farm, Horton Lane, Epsom, Surrey, KT19 8PT

WEB: www.hobbledown.com
TEL: 0843 289 4979
EMAIL: TheHobblers@hobbledown.com
COST: £££ (online discounts are available); children under 2 are free
OPENING TIMES: 10.00am–6.00pm/8.00pm daily
(closing time dependent on season, check website for up-to-date information). All outdoor equipment closes at dusk
AGE RANGE: 0–16
BABY CARE: change facilities available within the park
FOOD: Hobnosh restaurant, the Cabin café open during school holidays, or take a picnic
NEAREST STATION: Epsom station (overground trains from Clapham Junction), then catch the E9 bus

Hobbledown is a 50-acre adventure playground and children's farm on the outskirts of southwest London. Home to over 200 animals as well as indoor and outdoor play equipment, the park is based on a classic adventure story of riddles and rhymes written by AJ Kecojevic – a theme that is continued in every corner of the park, from the toilets and signage to the play space and staff.

Hobbledown is all about adventurous and challenging play, so be prepared for plenty of running, jumping, clambering for both you and the kids. Some of the high ropes and tunnels are large enough for adults, so you can really make the most of the time with the family and play along.

Outdoor, there are zip lines, high ropes (climbers are harnessed), huge bouncing pods, endless climbing equipment and tunnels, a great sand pit and a water play space. There is a Crystallite Mine – a play space of tunnels, hideouts, slides and water play – as well as Hobbledown Village and Hobbledown Market to explore. There are also two magical meadows – Field of Confusion and Wanderers Field for little legs to run free. For rainy days, there is a huge 1,115 square metre (12,000 square foot) indoor play barn with soft play areas, climbing equipment, scramble nets, tunnels, ball cannons… and more.

In school holidays there are often special activities for kids – story time, puppet shows and outdoor theatre – so check the website or give them a call to check what's on during your visit.

As well as the indoor and outdoor play space there are farm animals including pigs, goats, sheep, chickens, rabbits, donkeys, peacocks, geese, cows and Shetland ponies. There are also more exotic animals such as meerkats, llamas, parrots, chipmunks, otters, chinchilla, wallabies, and rhea. A petting corner is open during weekends and school holidays for children to get up close with the animals. Hobbledown regularly put on bird

displays for visitors to see their huge birds of prey in full flight, and there are plenty of animal talks happening throughout the day.

There is plenty of picnic space, as well as a café that serves healthy kid-friendly drinks, meals, snacks and coffee. They also sell picnic bags for anyone wishing to take their lunch into the meadows.

As one of London's better adventure playgrounds it is very well looked after and the attention to detail doesn't go unnoticed. Lockers are provided for bags, the entrance system is simple and helpful staff are spread throughout the park making this an easy and enjoyable playground for parents… and the kids love it.

As it is built for children and adults to play together, adults cannot enter without a child, and vice versa, children cannot enter or leave without an accompanying adult.

Kensington Palace

Kensington, London, W8 4PX

WEB:	www.hrp.org.uk
TEL:	+44 (0) 20 3166 6000
EMAIL:	kensingtonpalace@hrp.org.uk
COST:	££££ (online discounts available); children under 16 are free
OPENING TIMES:	10.00am–5.00pm/6.00pm (closing times dependent on season, check website for up-to-date information)
AGE RANGE:	3+
BABY CARE:	change facilities available, prams can be left in the cloakroom
FOOD:	The Orangery Café
NEAREST STATION:	High Street Kensington (District and Circle lines), Queensway (Central line)

An interesting alternative to Buckingham Palace, Kensington Palace has been an operating residence of the royal family since the 17th century. It was the birthplace of Queen Victoria and the one-time home of Diana, Princess of Wales. Today, it houses the apartments and offices for a number of the royal family, including the Duke and Duchess of Cambridge and Prince Harry.

Kensington Palace is simply beautiful to wander around. It is divided into themed sections, making it easy to visit. The Victorian area is the most popular exhibit, telling the story of the fascinating life of Queen Victoria – from her childhood hobbies and interests, her love for Albert, and her eventful and illustrious reign as queen. For the kids, the *Childhood and Family Life* room in the Victoria area has a wonderful toy box filled with traditional royal toys with which to play, and most rooms have something to entertain the younger visitors such as wooden puzzles and traditional paper spinners.

There are the opulent rooms of the King's State Apartments to explore – with the grand staircase, the Cupola Room, the King's Gallery, and the King's Drawing Room. The apartments hold many works of art from the Royal Collection, including tapestries, terracotta busts, carvings and paintings. One of the most famous paintings is of *Venus and Cupid* by Vasari, which hangs on the wall of the King's Drawing Room. There are also the Queen's State Apartments to see – the private rooms created for Queen Mary (wife of William of Orange) in the 17th century.

Kensington Palace has two free family trails to pick up at White Court ticket desk – one on the Victoria Revealed exhibition and one on the King's State Apartments. The website also has a number of printable activities for kids, such as making your own Queen Victoria puppet, or creating your own Georgian bonnet. And for ardent royalists,

the kids website www.hrp.org.uk/palacekids is full of quizzes, games, activities and videos for the family.

Kensington Palace is pram-friendly, with a lift provided to every floor. Prams can also be left in the cloakroom. Like all London museums, there are always special events and workshops for families during school holidays. Check the website for things happening during your visit.

As well as the Palace itself, Kensington Palace gardens are thoroughly enchanting and a great space for the whole family to explore. From the sunken garden, with its terraces, pond and ornamental flowerbeds, to the arched, tree-lined Cradle Walk walkway; the many shady corners and vibrant colours of flowers make the gardens an ideal choice on a summer's day. (Note, keep an eye on toddler and younger children, as the pond is not fenced and they could fall in.) Also in the gardens is the Orangery Café, which provides high chairs, serves children's meals, and even offers children's afternoon tea. They will also warm bottles.

Once you are finished at the Palace, there is the wonderful Diana Memorial Playground just outside (see page 102).

LEGOLAND® Windsor

Winkfield Road, Windsor, SL4 4AY

WEB:	www.legoland.co.uk
TEL:	0871 222 2001
COST:	££££ (online discounts available); children under 3 are free
OPENING TIMES:	10.00am–5.00pm/7.00pm (winter/summer), open March to November
AGE RANGE:	3–12
BABY CARE:	Baby Care Centre located in the first aid building; baby food for sale at the cafes
FOOD:	plenty of cafes serving full meals, lunch boxes and light snacks, or take a picnic
NEAREST STATION:	Windsor & Eton Central (Overground trains), Windor & Eton Riverside (Overground trains), and catch a shuttle bus from either station

For all those parents that understand the pain of a rogue piece of LEGO lurking amidst the carpet, LEGOLAND is a perfect antidote and the ideal place to set your resident little block-scatterer free. A theme park designed for children aged 3–12, LEGOLAND houses 55 interactive rides, as well as shows, workshops and play space to delight every LEGO fan.

The park is split into 11 themed lands, each with it's own set of attractions. Miniland is the place where the master builders thrive, with almost 40 million pieces of LEGO used to recreate a number of well-known cityscapes, complete with cars, boats and sound effects.

DUPLO® Valley is a great space for the tiny tots, with two huge water play areas – Drench Towers and Splash Safari as well as the Fairy Tale Brook, DUPLO Train, Brickville play space, DUPLO Theatre and DUPLO Valley Airport.

The Traffic area is where kids can climb aboard a range of LEGO-themed vehicles – the Boating School, the Balloon School, the L-Drivers electric cars (for 3–5 years), and the Driving School (for 6–13 years)… they can even join the LEGO fire brigade at the Fire Academy.

LEGO City has fun activities with remote control trucks, the Xbox gaming Zone, the Digger Challenge, or all aboard the Orient Expedition on a quest through crocodile-infested lands. There is also a pirate-themed live action show; see website for up-to-date times.

Adventure Land is where kids can try their hand at the climbing wall, go on a dinosaur safari, get soaked on the jet-ski pods, or venture under the sea on a submarine voyage.

Kingdom of the Pharaohs is where you'll find typical theme park rides, with a Desert Chase carousel, Aero Nomad Ferris wheel, a Laser Raider ride, a flying chair ride, and a 15-foot Scarab-bouncer.

Other areas include the Pirate Shores, with a range of swashbuckling activities, Knights Kingdom for those budding knights to chase dragons, and Land of the Vikings, with some rides for the bigger kids such as a giant river splash, spinning tops, a labyrinth, and pirate ship.

As well as the many outdoor attractions, LEGOLAND also has a huge Imagination Centre, where children (and adults!) can build whatever their imagination allows at the many building tables in the Discovery Zone; there are even workshops for anyone looking for building tips. There is also the Imagination Theatre where you can see a range of short 4D movies (up-to-date screening times are on the website).

LEGOLAND can get very busy during school holidays, so try and visit out of peak times or be prepared to queue for the popular rides on busy days. The park has introduced a system called Q-Bot, which allows visitors to reserve a space in a queue while doing something different in the park (for an extra fee), this can be booked online or when you arrive.

London Duck Tours

Duck stop, next to the London Eye, London, SE1 7PB

WEB:	www.londonducktours.co.uk
TEL:	+44 (0) 207 928 3132
COST:	£££; children under 12 months are free
OPENING TIMES:	10.00am–3.00pm/5.50pm (closing times dependent on season)
AGE RANGE:	3+
NEAREST STATION:	Waterloo (Jubilee, Northern and Bakerloo lines), Westminster (Jubilee, District and Circle lines)

If you are considering taking a tour of London, but not sure whether the kids will sit still for the duration, Duck Tours provide child-friendly tours that are fun, exciting and a completely unique way of seeing London's sites.

All tours are taken aboard one of their rather quirky, and very distinctive yellow amphibious vehicles – spending some time on the streets of London, and some travelling along the River Thames. The half truck, half boat vehicles originate from the Second World War, when they played a vital role in the Allied invasions. The name originates from the code-name DUKW: D is the first year of production code ('D' for 1942), U is for the body style of utility truck, K is for front wheel drive, W represents the two rear driving wheels. These rare vehicles have been completely rebuilt by Duck Tours for use on the roads today; each Duck carries 30 passengers.

London Duck Tours offer a number of routes, each covering a different area of London. Their *Classic Tour* takes in sights such as the London Eye, Houses of Parliament, Downing Street, Nelson's Column, St James's Palace, Buckingham Palace, Westminster Abbey, and MI6. Their *D-Day Duck Tour* includes St Paul's Cathedral, RAF Church, Blitz tube station, Trafalgar Square, Buckingham Palace, Churchill War Rooms, Houses of Parliament, MI5, MI6 and the Imperial War Museum. The *James Bond Tour* includes the Houses of Parliament, Ian Fleming's Office, Nelson's Column, Odd Job's Bowler Hat Shop, M's Club, Buckingham Palace, Q's Office, MI5 and MI6. And the *City Tour* includes Fleet Street, Bank of England, Tower of London, the Shard, Southwark Cathedral, MI6, Houses of Parliament, Lambeth Palace and the London Eye.

All tours have commentary from a tour guide that is sure to keep everyone entertained, with plenty of interesting facts, trivia and humour along the way. Tours last about 75 minutes with approximately 30 minutes on the water; all tours pick up

from their stop near the London Eye. You can book ahead online or get tickets from the booking office, also by the London Eye. The first tour departs at 10.00am and tours are spaced at regular intervals throughout the day.

The tours are generally recommended for those over the age of 3; babies under 12 months can travel for free.

London Eye

Riverside Building, County Hall, Westminster Bridge Road, London, SE1 7PB

WEB:	www.londoneye.com
TEL:	+44 (0)871 781 3000
COST:	£££££ (online discounts available); children under 4 are free
OPENING TIMES:	10.00am–8.30pm/9.30pm
AGE RANGE:	all ages
BABY CARE:	change facilities located in the main ticket hall
FOOD:	nothing on site, but several cafes along the Southbank
NEAREST STATION:	Waterloo (Jubilee, Northern and Bakerloo lines), Westminster (Jubilee, District and Circle lines)

Also known as the Millennium Wheel (due to it being erected in celebration of the Millennium in London), the London Eye is essentially a huge Ferris wheel, on the Southbank of the River Thames. Currently Europe's tallest Ferris wheel, it is 135 metres (443 feet) tall and 120 metres (394 feet) wide. It did offer the highest viewpoint of London until the viewing observatory at the Shard opened in 2012 (see page 42 for more details).

The London Eye has 32 air-conditioned capsules in which passengers ride that are attached to the external rim of the giant wheel, each capsule holding up to 25 people. You can walk around inside the pod as the wheel slowly rotates, but there is also seating in the middle.

The wheel rotates at 26 cm (10 inches) per second, so is slow enough that you can't really feel it going around, and it doesn't need to stop to allow people on or off (though it can be stopped if necessary for disabled or elderly passengers). It takes around 30 minutes to do one full revolution of the wheel, but you should allow plenty of extra time for queues beforehand.

Before you embark on the ride, there is the entertaining 4D experience – a 3D film with in-theatre effects that tells the story of a girl in London who takes a ride on the London Eye. Fireworks feature at the end of the film. (Note, this part of the experience is not recommended for children under the age of 2 years old as it contains strobe lighting.)

The website has a mobile app available for download prior to your visit to enhance your experience on the London Eye, offering 3D panoramas from the highest points as well as other additional information.

The wheel itself is quite a feat of engineering. Constructed in sections that were floated up the river on barges, it was assembled lying flat and gradually raised at a

rate of 2 degrees per hour, until it stood upright. Supported on one side by an A-frame, it is described by the operators as 'the worlds tallest cantilevered observation wheel'. The London Eye is now the most popular paid tourist attraction in the UK, hosting more than 3.5 million passengers every year.

London Transport Museum

Covent Garden Piazza, London, WC2E 7BB

WEB:	www.ltmuseum.co.uk
TEL:	+44 (0) 20 7379 6344
EMAIL:	bookings@ltmuseum.co.uk
COST:	££££; children are free
OPENING TIMES:	10.00am–6.00pm daily (last entry 5.15pm)
AGE RANGE:	all ages
BABY CARE:	change facilities on the ground floor, free cloakroom
FOOD:	2 cafes with high chairs, and a picnic area
NEAREST STATION:	Covent Garden, Leicester Square (Piccadilly line), Embankment (District and Circle lines), Charing Cross (Northern and Bakerloo lines)

Tucked away in the corner of Covent Garden, this understated museum exhibiting the history of London's famous transport network is full of interactive displays and activities for the kids… as well as plenty of interesting facts for the grown ups.

The collection began at the beginning of the 20th century, with a number of buses that were retired from service. It gradually grew to include rail vehicles, trams, trolley buses from the 19th and 20th centuries, and related artefacts. The museum moved to its present site at Covent Garden in 1980.

The most significant exhibit is the first underground train, dating from 1890. You can climb on many of the exhibits; sit behind the wheel of a London bus, or be a passenger inside an old 'padded cell' train carriage.   During school holidays, the Transport Museum puts on a range of free workshops and activities for kids – storytelling, arts and crafts, and discovery. At weekends you can visit the Family Station to pick up a range of children's activities to enhance your visit as you explore the museum. From spotting shapes for the under 5s, to creating Flickr frames for the older kids, there is something for every age group.

There are two dedicated children's areas in the museum. For the under 6s there is the *All Aboard!* activity area on Level 0. With its range of mini vehicles, the younger ones can pretend to be a bus driver, a train driver, or even a taxi driver. There is also a great play space with miniature trains on a scale model of London where kids can drive the vehicles around the busy city streets. On level 1 is the *Interchange* area for ages 7 to 11. Here the older kids can try on replica costumes and uniforms and learn about the people who have worked on public transport. The museum also has a very popular shop that sells unique posters, books, model vehicles and gifts, and there is a lift to get prams between floors.

Summer Reading Challenge 2023

Ready,
Set,
Read!

Presented by The Reading Agency.
Delivered in partnership with libraries.

summerreadingchallenge.org.uk

Laila 5

Join the Summer Reading Challenge for loads of fun!

It's FREE to take part at the library. You'll read books over the summer and collect special stickers and rewards.

Could you skip, scoot or take the bus to the library? You could even play a game on the way!

Get ready to read!

YOUTH SPORT TRUST | INSPIRING ACTIVE READERS | THE READING AGENCY

summerreadingchallenge.org.uk

In all Bromley libraries

8th July – 2nd September

Free for children of all ages and reading abilities

Join in the fun and win a medal!

www.better.org.uk/libraries/bromley

In partnership with
Bromley

BETTER
the feel good place

There is a picnic space which offers a perfect child-safe space to stop for a snack, as well as two cafes inside the museum. But with Covent Garden on the doorstep, there are also plenty of options for lunch and other activities on the streets outside.

The London Transport Museum has another site at Acton called the Museum Depot, which holds everything not on display at the site in Covent Garden. It has open weekends twice a year when the public can visit the 370,000 objects in storage – check the website for times and dates.

London Zoo

Outer Circle, Regent's Park, London NW1 4RY

WEB:	www.zsl.org
TEL:	+44 (0) 20 7722 3333
EMAIL:	marketing@zsl.org
COST:	££££ (online discounts available)
OPENING TIMES:	10.00am–4.00pm/6.00pm (closing times vary dependent on season, check website for current times)
AGE RANGE:	all ages
BABY CARE:	change facilities available in accessible toilets
FOOD:	café, restaurant and a kiosk, all serving healthy options, or there's plenty of space for a picnic in Regent's Park
NEAREST STATION:	Camden Town (Northern line)

Set in beautiful Regent's Park, London Zoo was the world's first scientific zoo. Opened in 1827, it is home to the Zoological Society of London, whose mission is to promote and achieve the worldwide conservation of animals and their habitats through long-term breeding programs, science and education. Today, London Zoo is home to more than 750 animal species – making it one of the largest collections in the UK – as well as a fabulous range of interactive experiences and live shows.

The zoo is split into 17 animal areas to explore. The Gorilla Kingdom is one of the most popular, with a trail that winds through the African forest environment to see western lowland gorillas, colobus monkeys and other African animals. Tiger Territory is also fabulous, with the opportunity to come face to face with the tigers – including the endangered Sumatrans – through the floor-to-ceiling glass window.

Another favourite for the whole family is Penguin Beach, with fabulous underwater viewing areas from which to observe a colony of Humboldt penguins. The area is also a breeding facility with a penguin nursery and pool where the young penguins learn to swim. Penguins are fed twice a day. Check the website for details.

Other animal exhibits include: pygmy hippos, four impressive Galapagos tortoises, otters, butterflies, a reptile house, a splendid aviary with more than 100 species of birds, and an African exhibit with some of Africa's most unusual animals.

There is also an extensive children's zoo where children can get up close and feed the animals and learn more about the animal kingdom. The children's zoo includes three zones: The Tree Top Zone where kids can climb the lookout towers for a treetop view of the zoo; the Roots Zone, where a network of tunnels lets kids explore an underground world; and a Splash Zone, where kids can learn about the importance of water to life on Earth.

London Zoo offers a number of experiences that allow kids to get up close with the animals. In the expert care of the animal keepers, kids can choose to meet penguins, meerkats, giraffes, kangaroos or owls. For any budding zoo keepers, the zoo also offers a 'junior keeper for a day' experience, where kids can really get to see what goes on behind the scenes, taking part in essential animal care and getting really close to some of the most loved animals. These experiences have an extra charge and can be purchased online or at the gate. Check the website for bookings and times.

The world's first aquarium was opened at London Zoo in 1853 (the word aquarium was actually invented here). The aquarium moved to its current location in the zoo in 1924, with three halls dedicated to some of the world's most exotic underwater creatures including piranhas, reef fish and freshwater fish. The zoo also has a significant seahorse breeding program.

Pollock's Toy Museum

1 Scala Street, London, W1T 2HL

WEB:	www.pollocksmuseum.co.uk
TEL:	+44 (0) 20 76363452
EMAIL:	info@pollocksmuseum.co.uk
COST:	£££ (free entry as part of the London Pass, see page 172)
OPENING TIMES:	10.00am–5.00pm daily (last entry 30 minutes before closing)
AGE RANGE:	6+
BABY CARE:	none
FOOD:	none
NEAREST STATION:	Goodge Street (Northern line)

If you are looking for something completely different, Pollock's Toy Museum is a major slice of quirkiness tucked away in the back streets of Fitzrovia. Named after Benjamin Pollock, the famous printer of toy theatres, the museum is dedicated to traditional English toys. Set up in an old terrace house, this unusual museum is a treasure trove of weird and wonderful toys from the last 200 years. The series of dusty rooms and creaky narrow stairs take you back in time; when toys were all about imagination and magic.

The atmosphere in Pollock's Toy Museum is something that cannot be recreated – the whimsical charm, the nooks and crannies that are crammed with puppets, stages, theatres, doll houses and train sets.

Though it's probably not a place for younger children (there is nowhere for prams, no toilets, and some of the toys can actually look a bit scary!), for the older, more curious children, seeing so many toys from yesteryear could be the perfect antidote to the modern world for an hour - hopefully sparking the inspiration for more imaginative play.

There is a fabulous toy shop downstairs in the museum, or head to the well-known Pollock's Toy Shop in Covent Garden for a larger selection of traditional toys for sale.

Royal Observatory Greenwich

Blackheath Avenue, Greenwich, London, SE10 8XJ

WEB:	www.rmg.co.uk/royal-observatory
TEL:	+44 (0) 20 8858 4422
EMAIL:	bookings@rmg.co.uk
COST:	£££ entry to the Observatory is free, Flamsteed House has a charge (can be purchased as part of the Big Ticket, see page 172); there is an additional charge for the Planetarium; children under 5 are free
OPENING TIMES:	10.00am–5.00pm daily (last entry 30 minutes before closing)
AGE RANGE:	all ages
BABY CARE:	change facilities in the Maritime Museum nearby
FOOD:	several cafes, plenty of picnic space in Greenwich Park
NEAREST STATION:	Greenwich Station (DLR line), or, catch the riverboat from Westminster to Greenwich Pier

The Royal Observatory – at the top of the steep hill in the middle of Greenwich Park – is best known for being the home of the prime meridian line, where Greenwich Mean Time was founded in 1884.

At the Observatory you can explore the galleries and learn how the universe was formed, guide a space mission, touch a 4.5 billion-year-old meteorite, and use the camera obscura lens to see a real-time view of Greenwich. There is also an interesting display on the history of time, which includes a number of timepieces that tell the story of how accurate timekeeping became possible.

Also part of the Observatory complex is Flamsteed House. Designed by Christopher Wren in 1675, Flamsteed House is the original Observatory building at Greenwich. It includes the Time galleries and the Meridian Courtyard, where you can stand on the world-famous meridian line – Longitude 0°, which divides the eastern and western hemispheres of the Earth. Since the late 19th century, the Prime Meridian has served as the reference for Greenwich Mean Time (GMT), from which the whole world sets its clocks and was the official starting point for the new Millennium.

Flamsteed House is home to the great equatorial telescope. Built in 1893 and used for astronomical research until the 1960s, this telescope is the seventh largest in the world, and largest of its kind in the UK. High on top of Flamsteed House you will find the bright red time ball – one of the world's earliest public time signals. First used in 1833, at exactly 13.00 GMT (winter) and 13.00 BST (British summer time) the ball falls from the top of its mast to the bottom, signalling the precise time to the many Londoners and ships on the River Thames.

Also part of the Observatory is the Peter Harrison Planetarium. From a space safari for the under 7s, to a fantastic visual exploration of the dark universe, the planetarium

has shows throughout the day, aimed at different ages and interests. Check website for full listings of what is showing during your visit. Entry to the shows has an additional charge; tickets can be purchased at the door or ahead of time as part of the Big Ticket offer (see page 172).

SEA LIFE London Aquarium

County Hall, Westminster Bridge Road, London SE1 7PB

WEB:	www.visitsealife.com
TEL:	+44 (0)871 663 1678
EMAIL:	sllondon@merlinentertainments.biz
COST:	£££ (online discounts available); can be purchased as a Merlin combi ticket (see page 172); children under 3 are free
OPENING TIMES:	10am–7.00pm (last entry 6pm)
AGE RANGE:	All ages
BABY CARE:	change facilities available on every floor, buggy park available weekends and daily during school holidays; lift access to every level
FOOD:	No eating or drinking inside, but there are plenty of cafes nearby
NEAREST STATION:	Waterloo (Jubilee, Northern and Bakerloo lines), Westminster (Jubilee, District and Circle lines)

With over 500 species and over 2 million litres of water, SEA LIFE London Aquarium is the largest aquarium in London and home to one of the largest collections of marine life in Europe. It is located on the ground floor of the historic County Hall building, on the South Bank of the River Thames.

The aquarium is split into 14 themed zones across three floors, and visitors follow a very clear route through the attraction. The most notable display is the sharks, in which you can see more than 40 sharks from 12 different species. To view the sharks, the aquarium has both a glass walkway, called the Shark Walk, and a huge three-floor-high display called the Shark Encounter. There is also the interactive Shark Academy where you can touch sharkskin and learn all about these magnificent creatures.

SEA LIFE is home to the most endangered crocodile species on the planet – the Cuban crocodiles – as well as Green Sea Turtles from the tropical seas of the Pacific and Atlantic oceans. There are also stingrays, lobster, jellyfish, piranhas, coral and seahorses on display. In the Ice Adventure zone, you can visit the aquarium's colony

of Gentoo penguins. Full of interactive features visitors have a direct window into the penguin cave, as the little creatures dive and play beneath the water.

As well as the exhibitions, SEA LIFE offers diving displays and touch pools for visitors to get up close with the marine life. There is also a daily schedule of feeding times and talks. Talks cover a range of creatures including octopus, stingrays, penguins, sharks, coral, terrapins, seahorses and piranhas. The ray feed allows you to directly feed the creatures. Check the website for times during your visit.

For those brave enough, SEA LIFE offers visitors the opportunity to snorkel with the sharks, where participants can get within a few feet of sand tiger sharks, black tip reef sharks and brown sharks. The experience takes approximately 90 minutes and includes a behind the scenes tour, full briefing, all snorkel equipment (no diving experience necessary but you must be able to swim). This needs to be booked ahead and the snorkel experience includes priority entrance into the aquarium.

It takes about two hours to get around the whole aquarium, dependent on which feeding talks you go to, but allow longer for queues. SEA LIFE is a popular attraction and can get very crowded particularly on school holidays and weekends. Queuing with kids is never fun, so get there early, or book a priority entrance ticket online to jump the queues (combi tickets automatically include priority entrance, see page 172).

The View from The Shard

32 London Bridge Street, London, SE1 9SG

WEB:	www.theviewfromtheshard.com
TEL:	+44 (0) 84 4499 7111
EMAIL:	enquiries@theviewfromtheshard.com
COST:	££££ (online discounts available); children under 3 are free
OPENING TIMES:	10am–7.00pm/10.00pm (Nov–March/April–Oct)
AGE RANGE:	3+
BABY CARE:	visitor toilets in the booking hall, prams must be left downstairs
FOOD:	no eating or drinking inside, but there are plenty of cafes nearby
NEAREST STATION:	London Bridge (Jubilee and Northern lines)

For those with a head for heights, a trip up the Shard is top of the list. The Shard is Western Europe's tallest building and a seminal piece of modern architecture. The inspiration for the sloping glass facades came from the spires of London churches; the eight football-pitches' worth of glass reflecting the light as the summit tapers off, disappearing into the sky.

At approximately 309 metres (1,019 feet) high, it has been described as a 'vertical city' by the project's architect Renzo Piano. Now an iconic piece of London's skyline, the 95-storey glass-clad tower is home to several restaurants, a hotel, offices, apartments and retail space.

On floors 69–72 and 244 metres (800 feet) above street level is The View from the Shard. With staggering 360-degree views and being almost twice as high as any other vantage point in the city, it offers by far the best views of London. Visitors ascend to the lofty viewing galleries via high-speed lifts that cover the 69 floors in just 30 seconds. The viewing galleries are spread across three floors: the lower two of which are enclosed, while the upper level is open-air.

What really makes the view special is the digital 'Tell:scopes' that bring the

landmarks of London to life. Using digital touchscreens visitors simply point the camera at the landmark and the screen overlays the image with information about everything nearby. You can also use the screen to zoom in, zoom out, view the area at different times of the day... something that is really handy on an overcast day. Kids will love the fact that London below looks just like LEGO and though quite a pricey attraction, it really helps understand the scale of the city divided by the winding river below.

Tickets are timed, so make sure you are punctual. Once inside, you are free to spend as much time as you want there – for most with kids this is usually around an hour.

For the best experience you really need to visit on a clear day. On a good day, views of up to 64 km (40 miles) across the skyline are to be had. If the weather is particularly overcast, The View from The Shard guarantees that if you can't see at least three of the key landmarks – such as London Eye, St Paul's, and Tower Bridge – they will issue a ticket for every person to return on another day, within three months. You can also call their number on the day you plan to visit to check on the weather and the current visibility before turning up.

For those with prams, there are steps into the entrance of The Shard, and prams cannot be taken up to the viewing gallery; they can be left in the cloakrooms on the ground floor.

Tower Bridge Exhibition

Tower Bridge Road, London, SE1 2UP

WEB:	www.towerbridge.org.uk
TEL:	+44 (0)20 7403 3761
EMAIL:	enquiries@towerbridge.org.uk
COST:	££££ (online discounts available); can be used as part of the London Pass; children under 5 are free
OPENING TIMES:	10.00am–5.30pm/6.00pm (winter/ summer) Last admission 30 minuites prior to closing
AGE RANGE:	4+
FOOD:	none on site
NEAREST STATION:	London Bridge (Northern, Jubilee and overground lines)

Tower Bridge is one of London's most-loved icons and possibly the most famous bridge in the world. Opened in 1894, this suspension bridge, with its huge lifting roadways, has stood over the River Thames for more than 120 years.

The Tower Bridge Exhibition opened as a visitor attraction in 1982, offering the public a chance to explore this historical icon. To celebrate the bridge's 120th birthday, the exhibition was developed to include a glass walkway providing a bird's eye view of the bridge and passing traffic below.

On entry, kids can collect a Tower Bridge passport, which they can fill with stickers at each stop. There is also a Guy Fox Explore Kit that can be downloaded from the website and includes maps, puzzles and plenty to keep the kids interested. At the start of the exhibition is a short screening of the history of the bridge. And for any engineering fans there is a fascinating tour of the Victorian engine rooms, to see how the bridge works.

Access to the walkway is

© Angela Sutherland

© Barksy Media

via a lift; the exhibition is pram friendly. The walkway is about 60 metres (196 feet) long with a glass section in the middle. It is a little disconcerting to first step onto the glass, but each of the six glass panels can withstand the weight of an elephant and the whole walkway is supported by a carbon steel framework, so there is no need to worry. At 42 metres (138 feet) above street-level, you get fabulous panoramic views across London. The best time to visit is when the bridge is being lifted; these times vary but are always listed on the website. The bridge is raised around 850 times a year, to allow passing river traffic through.

To enhance the experience of the new walkway, Tower Bridge Exhibition launched an augmented reality app, which can be downloaded for free. The app provides visitors with a 360-degree view of the bridge lifting directly below your feet: just look for the QR codes on the floor to launch the videos. Don't worry if you get there and haven't had chance to get the app, staff on site have iPads to show the video to any visitors that would like to see them.

Tower of London

Tower Hill, London, EC3N 4AB

WEB:	www.hrp.org.uk/TowerOfLondon
TEL:	0844 482 7777
EMAIL:	toweroflondon.hrp.org.uk
COST:	£££ (attraction is included in the London Pass, see page 172); children under 5 go free
OPENING TIMES:	9.00am/10.00am–4.30pm/5.30pm (winter/summer – check website for up-to-date times)
AGE RANGE:	4+
BABY CARE:	change facilities in the accessible toilet in the New Armouries café; 2 buggy parks
FOOD:	New Armouries café, several kiosks, and space for a picnic
NEAREST STATION:	Tower Hill (District, Circle and DLR lines)

Steeped in 1,000 years of history, the Tower of London is a castle on the northern bank of the River Thames. Built in 1066, as part of the Norman Conquest, the castle has served as a royal residence, armory, treasury and prison. It was expanded under both Richard the Lionheart (reigned 1189-99) and Henry III (reigned 1216-72) to become a collection of towers and buildings surrounded by a large wall and moat; the original structures still remain. Notorious as a place of torture and execution, many key figures were sent here for imprisonment – Anne Boleyn, Sir Walter Raleigh, Guy Fawkes, Lady Jane Grey, even Queen Elizabeth I was imprisoned here before she became monarch. Prisoners were brought to the Tower by barge along the Thames and entered through Traitors' Gate, which is how the expression 'sent to the tower' originated. The Tower was again used as a prison and place of execution during the First and Second World Wars.

Today, the Tower of London is a leading tourist attraction and home to many different exhibitions and attractions. The most well known is probably the Crown Jewels – the priceless treasures of the monarchy. The jewels on display include the Imperial State Crown, St Edward's Crown, Queen Victoria's diamond crown, the Sovereign's Sceptre, as well as a staggering collection of gemstones such as the First Star of Africa – the largest flawless cut diamond in the world – the Stuart Sapphire, and Queen Elizabeth's pearls. Items such as the Imperial Crown are still used by the Queen today. The Crown Jewels are closely guarded by the Yeoman Warders, or 'Beefeaters', as they are nicknamed. The Yeoman Warders have been part of the Royal Bodyguard since the 1500s and can be found throughout the Tower of London, giving tours and standing guard.

One of the larger towers in the castle grounds is the White Tower. A stunning piece of Norman architecture, inside there is a lovely Romanesque chapel and the Royal Armouries collection.

Very popular with the kids is a walk atop the huge stone walls that encircle the castle, exploring the siege engines and discovering what makes the Tower of London such a formidable fortress. You can also wander through the Medieval Palace, where 13th-century life has been recreated in spectacular detail, or visit the Coins and Kings exhibit, which tells the 500-year story of the Royal Mint at the Tower of London. For those interested in the history of the British Infantry, the Fusilier Museum tells the story of the Royal Regiment of Fusiliers. The regiment was formed at the Tower in 1685 by King James II and still operates today. There is also a torture exhibition, but this is probably best avoided if you are travelling with younger children or those with a vivid imagination.

Other exhibitions include the Royal Beasts, which tells the story of the royal menagerie through a set of interactive displays. The royal menagerie is where wild and exotic animals such as lions, a polar bear, elephants, ostriches and kangaroos were held captive over a period of 600 years, from the early 1200s.

The huge ravens are a major piece of the history of the Tower. Legend says, 'If the ravens leave the Tower, the kingdom will fall' – and there are still seven ravens living at the Tower today. The ravens are fed daily by the Raven Master. See if you can spot them, but don't try to feed them; they can bite if they feel threatened.

The castle is ancient so parts of the walkways are cobbled and unsuitable for prams. There are several buggy parks around the castle, with two secure buggy parks next to the Salt Tower and Henry III's Watergate.

The website has plenty of resources to enhance a family visit to the Tower. From videos, online games, templates to make your own helmet, and for real royal fans there is the palace kids website www.hrp.org.uk/palacekids with games, quizzes and things to make and do.

Up! At The O2

The O2, Peninsula Square, London, SE10 0DX

WEB:	www.theo2.co.uk
TEL:	+44 (0) 844 856 0202
EMAIL:	boxoffice@upattheo2.co.uk
COST:	adult £££ (tickets must be booked in advance, limited time slots per day)
OPENING TIMES:	10am–6.00pm/10.00pm (closing time dependent on season)
AGE RANGE:	10+
NEAREST STATION:	North Greenwich (Jubilee line)

If you are travelling with kids older than 10 years and they love an expedition, Up! At The O2 is a great opportunity for bolder visitors to reach new heights, by climbing to the top of the O2 Arena (formally the Millennium Dome).

The Millennium Dome was built as part of the millennium celebrations as a monument to space and time – the circumference is 365 metres (days in the year), there are 12 masts (months in the year) and the summit of the walkway is 52 metres high (weeks in the year). Now a building of architectural significance in the UK, it is a well-known venue for concerts, exhibitions and events.

An unforgettable and quite novel experience, the guided climb takes you up and over the 190-metre (623-feet)-long tensile fabric walkway – a bit like walking on a giant trampoline. Dressed in full explorer attire (kids will feel like an astronaut), you are harnessed to the walkway for the whole time. The climb itself is a little steep, but it isn't difficult and there aren't any sheer drops, so there is no concern for vertigo from the more nervous climbers.

Don't forget your camera (though it needs to be small enough to fit in the pocket of the all-in-one suit), because from the observation deck, on a clear day you have spectacular 360-degree views up to 24 km (15 miles) across the skyline of London – of Greenwich, Canary Wharf, the Gherkin and along the river Thames. Also, the meridian line runs just to the left of the walkway. Though the viewpoint isn't the highest viewpoint in London, being outdoors on the rooftop of such an iconic building, makes it a unique, alternative and exhilarating way to take in the city skyline.

Climbs take place throughout the day and evening. For an atmospheric climb, try one at twilight as the city lights come on. The whole experience takes a couple of hours to complete, and there are plenty of places nearby serving food and drink.

At the O2 there are plenty of other attractions that will appeal to older kids. Pop into the Sky Studios, where you can go behind the scenes at the TV studio to see how the news is made, try the driving simulators at the Nissan Innovation Station, or head to CiniWorld @ The O2 to see a movie. If you are still feeling brave, catch the Emirates Cable Car (see page 16) across the river on your way home.

Warner Bros. Harry Potter™ Studio Tour

Studio Tour Drive, Leavesden, WD25 7LR

WEB:	www.wbstudiotour.co.uk
EMAIL:	via website
COST:	adult ££££ (tickets must be purchased in advance, no sales on the door); children under 4 are free
OPENING TIMES:	10am–4.00pm/6.30pm (closing time dependent on time of year)
AGE RANGE:	all ages
BABY CARE:	change facilities available in accessible toilets; cloakroom in the lobby for bags, coats and prams
FOOD:	Take a packed lunch, or there is a café on site
NEAREST STATION:	Watford Junction (Overground line from Euston) and catch a shuttle bus to the studio (see website for shuttle bus times)

The Warner Bros. Studio Tour London is a must-do for any Harry Potter fan visiting London. Located at the studios in Leavesden – 32 km (20 miles) north-west of London – the tour is based at the working studios where every Harry Potter film was made.

Opened in 2012, the Studio Tour offers a unique viewpoint on the magical film series. Taking you behind-the-scenes, visitors can see the sets, costumes and props that went into making the most successful film series of all time, discovering the animatronics and special effects that brought the many creatures to life.

Step through the gates of the Great Hall, stroll along the cobblestones and past the shopfronts of Diagon Alley; visit the Gryffindor common room and Dumbledore's office; take in 4 Privet Drive, ride a broomstick, and take a photo on Hagrid's motorbike. You can even enjoy a glass of butterbeer or a pack of Bertie Bott's Every Flavour Beans at the end of the tour.

Though an extra expense (at £5), the handheld digital guide is a nice addition, bringing the tour to life for the younger kids. Narrated by Draco Malfoy, it reveals some

closely guarded secrets behind the making of the movies, as well as interviews and exclusive behind-the-scenes footage.

Children can pick up their own free Activity Passport at the entrance. The Activity Passport includes a Golden Snitch and a booklet, in which to collect stamps along the way.

To avoid the tour being too busy, or copious queues at the door, entrance to the tour is staggered – you select your entry time when you purchase your ticket. The tour usually takes around 3–4 hours to get around.

For a family, this studio tour can get expensive very quickly, and the gift shop is no exception. But for any child that has loved the Harry Potter series, the experience is a magical one.

Windsor Castle

Windsor, Berkshire, SL4 1NJ

WEB:	www.royalcollection.org.uk
EMAIL:	bookinginfo@royalcollection.org.uk
COST:	££££ (entrance to the Great Kitchen is extra); children under 5 are free
OPENING TIMES:	9.45am–4.15pm/5.15pm (closing time dependent on season), last admission 1 hour prior to closing
AGE RANGE:	all ages
BABY CARE:	change facilities available in the courtyard and on the North Terrace; cloakroom is available for bulky bags; prams cannot be taken into the State Apartments
FOOD:	Take a packed lunch; food cannot be taken into the State Apartments or St George's Chapel, drinks and snacks available in the shop, cafes nearby in Windsor town
NEAREST STATION:	Windsor & Eton Central (Overground trains from Waterloo)

For those history fans hoping for a magical and quintessentially English castle, Windsor Castle is a must. The original castle was built in 1070 by William the Conqueror, and is the oldest and largest occupied castle in the world – having been home to a sovereign since the days of Henry I. Approximately 150 people live and work at Windsor Castle and the Queen is in residence many weekends. Because it is a royal residence, security is tight, so be ready with empty pockets and bags to be scanned on entry.

There are many things to see at Windsor Castle, and you can easily fill three hours here. Very popular with the kids is Queen Mary's Doll House, which was built for Queen Mary in 1924 by leading British architect Sir Edwin Lutyens. With running water, electricity, flushing toilets, working lifts and filled with thousands of miniature pieces, it is a perfect replica at a scale of 1:12 of an aristocratic home. From a fully stocked wine cellar to a library with shelves full of top literary works, the doll house is an incredible piece of history that kids will enjoy.

Another main attraction at Windsor Castle is St. George's Hall – an impressive room that is used for state banquets. The ceiling is filled with colourful coats of arms; see if you can spot those shields that have been left blank, legend says that they are the crests of disgraced knights.

The semi-state rooms, used by the Queen for official entertaining, are only open to the public in autumn and winter. These spectacularly lavish apartments, created for George IV, are some of the most richly decorated interiors in the Castle. The State Apartments are often used by members of the royal family today, and they hold some of the finest works of art from the Royal Collection.

Also, within the castle grounds is St. George's Chapel – a magnificent example of Gothic architecture and home to the tombs of Henry VIII, Jane Seymour and Charles I.

There are several activities to help families get the most out of their visit to Windsor Castle; all can be collected at the entrance. Firstly, there is a free family audio tour aimed at children aged 7–11, where magical characters that live at the castle guide you along your route. There is also a family activity trail that helps kids discover all of the magical secrets at the castle. Also available for download prior to your visit are a number of quiz sheets and themed trails: have one of the Queen's corgis be your guide in *A Royal Home*, discover the story of Queen Victoria with the *Queen Victoria at Windsor Castle* trail, and learn the secrets of castles with the *Learn about Castles* trail. The website also has a couple of educational games.

As well as the regular activities and events at the castle, during weekends and school holidays there are often special activities for school-aged children so check the website for things happening during your visit.

Windsor Castle is a great place to see the Changing of the Guard, which usually happens between 11.00 and 11.30am in the Castle's Lower Ward (check website for up-to-date schedules). It is similar to the one at Buckingham Palace, but often easier to navigate with children – it isn't quite as crowded but is still just as impressive.

If you aren't there to see the Changing of the Guard, the best time to visit Windsor Castle is early afternoon, after the coach tours that tend to arrive first thing have departed.

Note: there is no photography or video allowed in the State Apartments or St George's Chapel.

I've spent my pocket money

Things to do with kids that don't cost a penny

Visiting London doesn't have to be an expensive venture. This vibrant city is bursting at the seams with free child-orientated activities for the whole family to enjoy.

Barbican Big Adventure

Barbican Centre, Silk Street, London, EC2Y 8DS

WEB:	www.barbican.org.uk
TEL:	+44 (0)20 7638 4141
EMAIL:	education@barbican.org.uk
COST:	free
OPENING TIMES:	11.00am–6.00pm (Mon–Sat), 12.00pm–6.00pm (Sun & public holidays)
AGE RANGE:	6+
BABY CARE:	change facilities available in accessible toilets inside the Barbican Centre
FOOD:	several cafes in the Barbican Centre
NEAREST STATION:	Barbican (Metropolitan, Circle, Hammersmith & City lines)

For any daring detectives in the family, the Barbican Big Adventure is a fabulous way to spend a morning, discovering the secrets of the Barbican Centre by following a series of clues. This adventure trail takes visitors on a self-guided tour of the indoor and outdoor complex – scaling high walkways, past lakes and a waterfall, and through the conservatory to explore more than 2,000 species of plants and trees.

Aimed at children 6 years or older, the kids can lead the way throughout – it is a safe route that is clearly marked with attractive illustrations and numbered stops – and there are always Barbican staff on hand to help out if you get stuck. There are plenty of games to play along the way and fascinating facts to learn, as you complete puzzles and crack the code to unlock a prize.

The free trail kit can be picked up at the advance box office at the Barbican. The trail takes a minimum of one hour to complete, dependent on the number of people taking part and whether you stop along the way – at one of the art exhibitions, for lunch, or simply to take advantage of the open space for the kids to play. Remember to take along a pencil.

The Barbican Centre is a performing arts centre – the largest of its kind in Europe. It is home to the London Symphony Orchestra, the BBC Symphony Orchestra, and is the London venue for the Royal Shakespeare Company. It regularly hosts concerts, theatre performances and art exhibitions of all kinds as well as housing one of London's largest libraries and a conservatory. Aside from the Big Adventure, the Barbican often holds workshops and special events for kids, so check their website for things happening during your visit.

British Museum

44 Great Russell St, London, WC1B 3DG

WEB:	www.britishmuseum.org
TEL:	+44 (0) 20 7323 8299
EMAIL:	information@britishmuseum.org
COST:	free
OPENING TIMES:	10am–5.30pm
AGE RANGE:	4+
BABY CARE:	baby change facilities in the Great Court, the Clore Education Centre and the Ford Centre; fold up prams can be left for free in the cloakroom to the west of the main entrance
FOOD:	3 cafes, all with child-friendly food available, kids eat free at the Gallery Café, there is also a picnic area at the Ford Centre
NEAREST STATION:	Tottenham Court Rd (Central and Northern lines), Holborn (Central and Piccadilly lines), Russell Square (Piccadilly line)

Not only one of the world's oldest museums but also one of the world's best, the British Museum is a treasure trove of history and culture. With a permanent collection that numbers more than 8 million works from across the globe, the vast range of artefacts and activities span from as far back as the Mesopotamia era (6000–1500BC) to medieval Europe.

The museum is divided into easy-to-navigate galleries, each themed by its era and civilisation. Top of the list for most kids are the Ancient Egypt galleries, where you can see Egyptian mummies, sculptures – including the huge statue of Ramesses II and the Rosetta Stone – the tomb-chapel of Nebamun and a plethora of artefacts from this fascinating era. Other galleries include Ancient Greece and Rome, Asia – where you'll find the Chinese Tang tomb figures - Europe and the Middle East.

For visitors, the museum puts on object-handling sessions daily, led by volunteers who can knowledgeably explain the background of each as well as answer any questions.

The museum has a number of activity trails, set up to bring the museum to life for younger visitors. Covering a number of topics and age groups – from chasing rainbows, or sailing down the Nile to travelling through time – each trail takes 30–40 minutes to complete. On weekends and during school holidays, the museum also offers free gallery backpacks (just pay a £10 refundable deposit), each with age-specific and era specific activities. Choose to go on an African adventure and make an animal mask, write your name in hieroglyphs in Ancient Egypt, craft a mosaic in Roman Britain, dress up as an ancient Greek, or become an archaeologist. Each activity backpack takes up to 90 minutes to complete. Visit the families desk in the Great Court for more details. If there is a budding artist in the family, this is also the place to pick up any art materials. Here you can borrow pencils, crayons and pads for sketching and colouring along the way.

If that isn't enough to keep the little ones entertained, the museum always has special family events happening throughout the year, just check the website for details close to your visit.

To supplement your visit, the museum also has a fantastic Young Explorers section on their website, with online games and activities, as well as interesting facts and stories about some of the artefacts found at the museum.

Hackey City Farm

1a Goldsmiths Row, London E2 8QA

WEB:	www.hackneycityfarm.co.uk
TEL:	+44 (0) 20 7729 6381
EMAIL:	farm@hackneycityfarm.co.uk
COST:	free (donations can be made at the entrance)
OPENING TIMES:	10am–4.30pm. Tuesday to Sunday, all year round
AGE RANGE:	All ages
BABY CARE:	change facilities available in accessible toilets
FOOD:	café on site
NEAREST STATION:	Hoxton (East London line) is a 10-minute walk, otherwise catch bus 26, 48 or 55 from central London

In the heart of east London, nestled next to Broadway Market, Hackney City Farm is a great opportunity for kids to experience life on a real farm. Visitors can get up close to a variety of livestock, with chickens, ducks and geese roaming freely (but don't get too close to the farm cats, they can sometimes be a bit scratchy). There are also sheep, pigs, donkeys and goats in enclosures, as well as rabbits and guinea pigs in hutches.

The farm shop sells fresh eggs and produce from the farm such as honey from the bees, and organic vegetables. There are also often stalls of local arts and crafts.

A quirky place, the farm is a vital part of the local community, offering sustainable farming vegetable boxes and bringing country spirit to the local area, so it is certainly a breath of fresh air from the frenetic city life that surrounds it.

There is a simple, inexpensive café that serves fresh Mediterranean-style meals so the farm is a great place to plan a food stop for breakfast or lunch, and the kids are sure to be delighted by the animals wandering by as they eat their food. There is also a lovely garden to wander through and stop for a rest, if little legs are getting tired.

There are often activities happening at Hackney City Farm, and you never know what you might stumble upon; the informal structure is something that just adds to the appeal. There could be an apple-pressing display, a jumble sale, a clothes swap, or a bike-mending workshop. Regular events include children's and adult's pottery classes, classes on low-impact living, and mosaic making. The website has a calendar of events and the twitter feed (@hackneycityfarm) also posts up-to-date details. You might even stumble on the odd tweet from Larry the Donkey!

Though it's not huge, it is a nice bite-sized farm with a family-friendly focus that allows you to escape the busy streets for a while and try something a bit different.

Horniman Museum and Gardens

100 London Road, Forest Hill, London, SE23 3PQ

WEB:	www.horniman.ac.uk
TEL:	+44 (0) 20 8699 1872
COST:	free
OPENING TIMES:	10.30am–17.30pm
AGE RANGE:	all ages
BABY CARE:	change facilities available in accessible toilets, baby-feeding room off Gallery Square; buggy park in Gallery Square
FOOD:	Horniman café within the museum, picnic area on the Bandstand Terrace
NEAREST STATION:	Forest Hill (Overground line) is a 5–10 minute walk, otherwise catch bus 176 from central London

A little off the beaten track, yet one of London's hidden gems, the Horniman Museum and Gardens is a fantastic slice of quirkiness, and possibly London's most child-friendly museum. With a little bit of everything – natural history, anthropology, musical instruments – as well as wonderful gardens, a petting zoo and an aquarium, it has plenty to keep kids of all ages entertained.

The Hands on Base is a space where visitors can immerse themselves in thousands of different artefacts – try on a Mexican mask, play an instrument from India, touch armour or stuffed animals. With plenty of space to run around and make noise, it is a sensory paradise for kids.

The musical instrument collection is a huge hit with kids. The largest display of its kind in the UK, there are 1,300 instruments on display, each with its own story. In particular, there is a display of keyboard instruments and a space where you can play instruments for yourself. There are also displays that tell stories of musical development around the world, how instruments have evolved and how instruments are made.

Other displays include the African Worlds Gallery, a Natural History Gallery, and a Centenary Gallery – all have plenty of interactive displays with buttons to push and things to touch.

From 12.30pm to 4pm the Animal Walk is

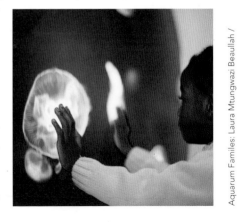

Aquarium Families: Laura Mtungwazi Beaullah / Horniman Museum & Gardens

Sound Gardens: Ludo des Cognets / Horniman Museum & Gardens

open, where visitors can be among a range of animals – alpacas, goats, sheep, guinea pigs, rabbits and chickens – and learn about the history of people and domesticated animals. While in the Nature Base, visitors can see a harvest mouse – Britain's smallest rodent – view the thousands of bees in the Horniman's beehive, and get hands on with the many nature-based activities.

The café, overlooking the gardens is reasonable and very child-friendly with plenty of healthy options, but the gardens are perfect for a picnic too.

There are activity packs available for download for each display, all well worth grabbing before you go. Yet with all of this on offer, often the most popular sight at the Horniman with the younger generations is the slightly bizarre giant stuffed walrus that you cannot miss.

Kentish Town Farm

1 Cressfield Close, off Grafton Rd, London, NW5 4BN

WEB:	www.ktcityfarm.org.uk
TEL:	+44 (0) 20 7916 5421
EMAIL:	ktcityfarm.org.uk
COST:	free to enter, activities are extra
OPENING TIMES:	9.00am–5.00pm
FOOD:	2 picnic areas
AGE RANGE:	all ages
BABY CARE:	baby change facilities in accessible toilet
NEAREST STATION:	Kentish Town (Northern and Overground lines), Gospel Oak (Overground line)

Kentish Town City Farm is the first of its kind in London. Nestled amidst the railway tracks of North London, it is a wonderful example of city farming – as horses trot under the arches and chickens squawk to the noise of the passing trains. There are frogs, horses, goats, pigs, geese, chickens, allotments and gardens… all of which you can wander around and lose yourself in. Kids can feed the animals, muck out the stables, or get involved in gardening. There is also an Under 5s activity room and plenty of garden space and seating areas.

Kentish Town Farm also has a pony-riding programme, which provides access to horses for children and those with special needs in the local area. Pony rides take place every Saturday and Sunday, and are available for children over the age of four, for just £2 per ride (check website for up-to-date times and prices).

There is always something happening at the farm for kids, with daily activities ranging from gardening, messy play, sing-alongs, art club, pottery club and baking. All activities are reasonably priced, ranging from £1-4 (check website for further details).

The farm has paths throughout so is easy to navigate for those with prams.

Mudchute Park & Farm

Pier Street, Isle of Dogs, London, E14 3HP

WEB:	www.mudchute.org
TEL:	+44 (0) 20 7515 5901
EMAIL:	info@mudchute.org
COST:	free, though donations are welcome at the door
OPENING TIMES:	09.00am–5.00pm daily.
AGE RANGE:	all ages
BABY CARE:	change facilities available in the toilets in the courtyard
FOOD:	Mudchute Kitchen with indoor and outdoor seating serves breakfast, snacks, sandwiches, and has a children's menu
NEAREST STATION:	Mudchute (DLR line)

Established in 1977, the 32-acre site of Mudchute Park and Farm is a wonderful example of urban meets country. Located in the middle of the Isle of Dogs, the park is one of the largest inner-city farms in Europe. Not a zoo, you walk right through the fields of sheep and cows as they graze against the rather bizarre backdrop of Canary Wharf.

With more than 100 animals and birds on the farm, many of them British rare breeds, the farm is one of the finest for those who want to really see farm animals. Throughout the farm you can see a huge range of breeds of cows, pigs, sheep, llamas, alpacas, as well as aviary birds, poultry and geese. In the Pets Corner, there are giant rabbits, guinea pigs and ferrets, many of which can be handled as part of an animal handling session. In the aviary you'll find a delightful range of budgerigars, cockatiels, golden pheasants and mandarin ducks. If you want to learn more about the animals, you can book a tour with one of the staff at the farm. Tours can be booked ahead of time through the website.

The café, on site, has a great selection of snacks and meals, as well as a decent children's menu. However, Mudchute Park is also a great spot for a picnic; a remarkable place where you can get spectacular views across London whilst sharing your lunch with the many feathered and furry creatures wandering around.

Though the farm is free, Mudchute is a community charity with donations from the public being the main source of income that keeps this wonderful site open. Spare change is appreciated at the gate.

Once you've had your fill of the Farm, there is a playground in Millwall Park, right next door to Mudchute Park.

Museum of London, City

150 London Wall, London EC2Y 5HN

WEB:	www.museumoflondon.org.uk
TEL:	+44 (0) 20 7001 9844
EMAIL:	info@museumoflondon.org.uk
COST:	free
OPENING TIMES:	10.00am–6.00pm
AGE RANGE:	All ages
BABY CARE:	change facilities on the entrance level
FOOD:	two cafes and a picnic area
NEAREST STATION:	St Pauls (Central line) (Metropolitan, Hammersmith & City and Circle lines)

The Museum of London has two sites in London that are both dedicated to the history of London. This city site focuses on the entire history of the city – from pre-Roman days to present day London.

Beginning with a display called *London before London*, visitors learn about the inhabitants of the area from 450,000 BC to the arrival of the Romans with historical artifacts and displays. There is an interesting Roman display that explains the road structures and the growth of the city as part of this dominant empire. The museum displays recount the collapse of the Roman city, before featuring a display of Medieval London that includes clothing, toys, paintings and jewellery. Then the *War, Plague and Fire Gallery* leads visitors though the turbulent Elizabethan times – including the Great Plague, the Great Fire of 1666, and the Civil Wars.

The museum then goes on to document the growth of the city from 1666 onwards. England is becoming a vast empire and London – as a trading capital – is a key piece of this expansion. On display are artefacts such as Nelson's sword, as well as an original 18th century Wellclose Square Prison cell, complete with contemporary graffiti written by doomed prisoners. From the 1850s onwards, the museum tracks the history of London as it becomes a city of social divide – documenting the increasing gap between rich and poor, the differing political landscapes, the suffragettes, and the onset of the First World War. These differences are starkly depicted in each of the galleries.

Not just focused on the past, the museum also takes a look at what we can expect for London in the future, with an interactive flowing river to spark debate on the changing face of the city, climate change and population density. The most popular exhibit at the museum is possibly the resplendent and hugely iconic Lord Mayor's Coach.

This city museum also hosts storytime, and play and explore events for the under 5s every week – check website for up-to-date times.

Museum of London, Docklands

West India Quay, London E14 4AL

WEB:	www.museumoflondon.org.uk/docklands
TEL:	+44 (0)20 7001 9844
EMAIL:	info@docklands@museumoflondon.org.uk
COST:	free
OPENING TIMES:	10.00am–6.00pm
AGE RANGE:	all ages; soft-play area for under 5s
BABY CARE:	change facilities on the entrance level
FOOD:	café on the entrance level; picnic area available
NEAREST STATION:	West India Quay (DLR), Canary Wharf (Jubilee line and DLR)

The second site for the Museum of London, this Canary Wharf location focuses on the history of the London port, from Roman times through to the height of trade and riverside commerce in the 1940s.

Beginning with the arrival of the Romans in AD43, the museum follows the growth of the area as early riverside trading settlements spring up. There are multimedia points to explain the history and a fabulous scale model of the Old London Bridge, which was the first stone structure to span the River Thames.

From here the museum tracks the growth of the British Empire through trade, with displays on the first wet docks, shipbuilding and a touchscreen journey aboard an East India cargo ship, depicting the perilous journey undertaken by the sailors.

The Sailortown Gallery is a fabulous recreation of 19th century London streets; an era when the lanes and alleys were a dark and winding maze. Here visitors can explore an alehouse, experience sailors' lodging house and much more.

There is an interesting display on the Second World War, a time when many of the docks were destroyed. There is also a life-size replica of a wartime shelter and exhibits on events such as the port's role in the Dunkirk rescue.

Bringing you up to the present day, the museum's final gallery examines the regeneration of the area, from the derelict port of the 1960s to the redevelopment of Canary Wharf as it stands today.

The Docklands museum also has a great soft play area for the under 5s, called the Mudlarks Children's Gallery. An interactive play area, it brings the history of London Docklands to life, with hands-on activities such as digging for treasure and climbing aboard a DLR train.

National Maritime Museum

Romney Road, Greenwich, London SE10 9NF

WEB:	www.rmg.co.uk/national-maritime-museum
TEL:	+44 (0) 20 8312 6565
EMAIL:	bookings@nmm.ac.uk
COST:	free (there is a charge for some exhibitions)
OPENING TIMES:	10.00am–5.00pm daily (last entry 30 minutes before closing)
AGE RANGE:	all ages
BABY CARE:	change facilities on lower ground, ground and first floors
FOOD:	several cafes, plenty of picnic space in Greenwich Park
NEAREST STATION:	Cutty Sark (DLR line) or, catch the riverboat from Westminster to Greenwich Pier

Greenwich has been synonymous with sea and navigation for centuries. It was a landing place for the Romans, and later the Royal Navy College housed along the banks of the River Thames nearby became home to the Royal Navy and Royal Navy training from 1873 to 1998.

The Maritime Museum was officially opened in 1934, and backs onto Greenwich Royal Park (see 104). Now part of the Royal Museums Greenwich, which includes the Queen's House, the Cutty Sark (see page 14), the Royal Observatory and Peter Harrison Planetarium (see page 38), the Maritime Museum is the leading maritime museum in England and the largest maritime museum in the world.

Telling the story of more than 500 years of British life at sea, the vast collection of more than 2 million maritime artefacts and interactive displays are enough to keep the most inquisitive of minds engaged. Displays include Nelson's uniform from the Battle of Trafalgar, a stunning collection of maritime art, ship models and plans, navigational equipment and manuscripts.

In the Children's Gallery, kids can become captain and steer a ship into port in the ship simulator – an interactive bridge that brings to life the hazards of the sea, and teaches about navigation and naval communication along the way. The simulator uses real equipment to take visitors through a number of scenarios – a fishing boat out at sea, a ferry in the port, or a naval rescue mission. Visitors can also load cargo in the port, hoist the sails, or test the meals the sailors ate, as they explore the ship *Seahorse*. There is also a hugely popular interactive game here, where kids can fire a cannon at pirates.

The Great Map offers a multi-sensory display. Here you can walk across the map, use touch screens to explore distant lands, play games, leap into the collections and discover all the treasures of the museum.

Next door to the Maritime Museum is the Queen's House, for which entry is also free. This stunning 17th century house was originally the home of Henrietta Maria, the queen of Charles I. Now it is home to an impressive fine-art collection.

In front of the Maritime Museum, towards the pier, there is the Discover Greenwich Visitors Centre. Here you will find information on things to do in the locality as well as a few interactive maritime displays and baby change facilities.

As the National Maritime Museum is part of the Royal Museums Greenwich, you can easily combine this visit with other attractions in the area.

National Portrait Gallery

St Martin's Place, London, WC2H 0HE

WEB:	www.npg.org.uk
TEL:	+44 (0) 20 7306 0055
EMAIL:	dsaywell@npg.org.uk
COST:	free
OPENING TIMES:	10.00am–6.00pm, open until 9.00pm Thursday and Friday
FOOD:	Portrait Café, which offers kids' lunchboxes on weekends and during school holidays
AGE RANGE:	6+
BABY CARE:	baby change facilities on level –2, –3 and 3
NEAREST STATION:	Leicester Square (Northern and Piccadilly lines), Charing Cross (Northern, Bakerloo and Overground lines)

Founded in 1856, the National Portrait Gallery is now home to more than 200,000 portraits. From the Tudor monarchs to Woody Allen, there are artworks of every shape, size and era to view. Though many would think a Portrait Gallery would be a stuffy affair, the National Portrait Gallery has done a great job of making art accessible to the whole family. Every portrait has a story, and with these stories, art and history can come alive.

A lot of this information is displayed alongside the artworks, but for the 7–11 year olds, there are themed interactive tours available (£4 for two audio players), that lead you through the exhibits providing fascinating facts and stories along the way.

On the ground floor you'll find the digital space where visitors have access to the Portrait Explorer – with which you can create your own tour, watch artist interviews, explore archival documents and timelines. You'll also find contemporary portraits and commissions. The first floor is where you'll find portraits of Queen Victoria, as well as late Victorian arts. The second floor houses art from 17th, 18th and 19th centuries: the Tudor Galleries, the Stuarts, Science and Industry, Royalty Celebrity and Scandal, and the Romantics.

Their exhibitions often rotate and change, so grab a map on the way in (or download from the website) for up-to-date exhibitions.

To keep the family interested, head to the Family Activity Base (open 11.00am–4.00pm every weekend) where you can pick up resources and materials to bring the museum to life for the younger visitors including a free sketchpad, and a pop-up gallery to fill with drawings.

The National Portrait Gallery also offers a free drop-in session every Sunday where families can take part in art workshops and activities. These cover a huge range of subjects and medias including sound and vision, photography, painting, drawing and animation, and for differing age groups. Check the website for details of what is happening during your visit. Some have limited capacity and require a free ticket (which can be picked up at the entrance). Again, check the website for more details on each workshop.

Natural History Museum

Cromwell Road, London, SW7 5BD

WEB:	www.nhm.ac.uk
TEL:	+44 (0) 20 7942 5000
EMAIL:	info@nhm.ac.uk
COST:	free (there is a charge for some exhibitions)
OPENING TIMES:	10.00am–5.50pm daily.
AGE RANGE:	all ages
BABY CARE:	baby-change rooms on lower ground floor and ground floor
FOOD:	several snack bars and cafes throughout the museum
NEAREST STATION:	South Kensington (Piccadilly and District & Circle lines)

One of London's most famous museums, the Natural History Museum is a 'must see' for anyone visiting the city with kids. The amount of displays is staggering and there is never enough time to see everything. From the moment you enter the Grand Hall and are met by the enormous skeleton currently on display, there is never a dull moment, with interactive displays at every turn.

To ensure it isn't overwhelming, the museum is laid out in very user-friendly colour coded zones. The Green Zone includes the creepy crawlies, the ecology area, a cross section of a giant sequoia, and an incredible collection of stuffed birds. It is also where you'll find the Investigate area where kids can touch meteorites, dinosaur bones and hundreds of other geological treasures.

The Red Zone is the Earth zone, which includes the fabulous Volcanoes and Earthquakes Gallery. Here you will find the famous earthquake simulator – a room that visitors can stand in and experience what it really feels like to be in an earthquake. The Red Zone also houses the Restless Surface Gallery that demonstrates how mountain ranges such as the Himalayas were formed, the Earth Lab, which is bursting with fossils to investigate, as well as a huge gallery of minerals, gems and rocks.

The Blue Zone explores the incredible diversity of life on the planet – from the blue whale to fishes, reptiles to marine invertebrates. It is also where you'll find the incredibly popular dinosaur exhibition. Finally, the Orange Zone includes the Darwin Centre and Attenborough Studio, which offer a daily programme of live animal encounters, scientist-led talks, films and many more experiences (check the website for more details). The Orange Zone is also home to the Wildlife Garden – a tranquil haven for thousands of plants and habitats, including woodland and meadow habitats (open from 1 April to 30 October).

The museum offers free Explorer backpacks designed for children under 7 to help them explore the museum. The backpacks contain an activity booklet, explorer binoculars and hat, and cover a variety of topics – birds, mammals, monsters, nature, and oceans.

There are stacks of other daily events happening around the museum – puppet shows, workshops, storytelling and more – so check the event calendar on the website before you go. Get there early, as there are often queues to get in. It is especially busy during school holidays and weekends. Because it is so popular, there is also sometimes a separate queue to get into the dinosaur exhibition.

Oasis Children's Venture

Larkhall Lane, Stockwell, London, SW8 2PD

WEB:	www.oasisplay.org.uk
TEL:	+44 (0) 20 7622 8756
EMAIL:	info@oasisplay.org.uk
COST:	adventure playground and nature garden are free; go-karting is £10 per session
OPENING TIMES:	adventure play: 3.30–6.00pm Tues–Fri, 10.30am–4.00pm Sat; go-kart track: 4.30–6.30pm Wed, Thurs, Fri, Sat; nature garden: 3.30–5.30pm, Mon–Fri.
FOOD:	bring your own
AGE RANGE:	adventure play: 6–16; go-kart track: 8+; nature garden: 5–16.
NEAREST STATION:	Stockwell (Victoria and Northern lines)

Oasis Children's Venture is a community project that offers three unique play facilities for children in the local area.

The Oasis adventure playground is a fabulous supervised play space for children from 6–16. It has a mountain bike track through the woods, an area for ball sports, a stack of equipment to play on including a zip line, climbing frames, swings, rock climbing wall, sand pit and natural play area. With a capacity of 50 children, the playground can get busy, so arrive early to ensure a space. Otherwise phone ahead to see how busy it is, though they can't book a space you can find out whether to expect a queue.

The Oasis go-kart track is a youth-led program that offers go-karting for children over the age of 8. The site is set up for both disabled and able-bodied drivers, and has dual-control cars. This section of the playground has a fee per session.

Across the road from the playground, is the Oasis nature garden. Designed for children from ages 5–14, the centre offers a range of environmental-based arts and crafts – from woodworking and growing vegetables, to going on a bug safari and building a den. Though it's in the heart of urban London, the nature garden has woods, a vegetable patch, a meadow and ponds for visitors to explore. A fantastic space for environmental education, the Oasis Children's Venture is a slice of nature in the heart of local London.

Regent's Canal Walk

Little Venice to Camden Lock

COST:	free
OPENING TIMES:	always open
FOOD:	bring your own
AGE RANGE:	all ages, younger ones will require a pram
NEAREST STATION:	Little Venice – Warwick Avenue (Bakerloo line). Camden Lock – Camden Town (Northern line)

One of the best ways to see London is to take a walk along the Regent's Canal. Offering a completely different view of the city, the canal winds its way through London, from Paddington to Limehouse.

An achievable section with kids is the stretch from Little Venice to Camden. Little Venice is a canal basin where the canal splits for Paddington, Limehouse, and heads

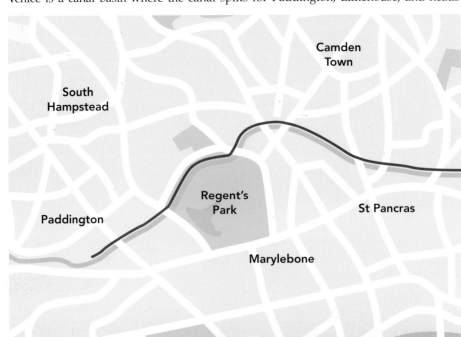

out of London to the West Midlands. It is a truly lovely part of the city, with grand townhouses along the water's edge and ducks, geese and cormorants nesting on the island in the middle of the canal. Along the towpath at Little Venice there is often a floating café and a floating art gallery. From here, the towpath toward Camden is edged with attractively maintained houseboats, many with their own little gardens. You'll pass through tunnels until you reach the top of Regent's Park, where the stunning white villas that surround the park also edge the canal. The canal also passes through the middle of London Zoo; though you can't see many animals, you walk right past the aviary. The path then continues on to Camden Lock, where there is both the operating canal lock alongside the famous Camden markets.

The markets can get busy but if you are brave enough and the kids can handle crowds, they are worth a quick peek. Here you'll find quirky stalls selling everything from handmade jewellery to puppets and wind chimes; there are plenty of food stalls too.

If you want to walk further, the canal continues on to the East End of London. This stretch is quieter, but still a pleasant walk as it passes many art galleries and houseboats and you'll see plenty more ducks and geese along the way. At Kings Cross, the canal passes the London Canal Museum that tells the history of the canal, from its industrial roots to present day. Entrance is £4 for adults, £2 for children.

If you don't fancy walking, you can take a boat trip along the same stretch of canal for around £9 for an adult, and £8 for a child one-way. See www.londonwaterbus.co.uk for timetables and further details.

The Roof Gardens in Kensington

99 Kensington High Street, London, W8 5SA (access via Derry Street)

WEB:	www.virginlimitededition.com/en/the-roof-gardens
TEL:	+44 (0) 20 7937 7994
EMAIL:	enquiries@virginlimitededition.com
COST:	free
OPENING TIMES:	9.00am–5.00pm daily (check availability prior, the space is often booked for private functions)
AGE RANGE:	all ages
FOOD:	Babylon Restaurant on Level 7, which is upmarket but does have a kids' menu, or space for a picnic within the gardens
NEAREST STATION:	High Street Kensington (District and Circle line)

Not to be confused with Kensington Gardens, The Roof Gardens in Kensington are the largest roof gardens in Europe and a marvel of urban gardening. Constructed amidst the Kensington skyline on the 1.5-acre rooftop of a department store, you would never imagine what is up above from the street below.

The Roof Gardens were the dream of Trevor Bowen, Vice President of John Barker & Co. In 1936, he hired talented landscape gardener Ralph Hancock to make it a reality. The gardens were constructed from more than 500 species of plants, with a soil-depth of just 45 cm (18 inches). The gardens were officially opened to the public in 1938.

Today, the gardens consist of three themed spaces. The Spanish Garden has delightful vine-covered walkways, fountains and a sun pavilion, all which instantly transport you from the busy streets below to a Mediterranean sanctuary. The Tudor Garden is made up of three courtyards that represent life in Tudor England. As a smaller walled garden with secret corners and spectacular view across west London, the Tudor Garden is a lovely place to sit for a picnic amid the fragrant lavender and roses. In the winter, this garden is planted with a seasonal garden and covered with a marquee, so it can be used all-year-round.

The English Woodland Garden is home to a huge variety of trees, including seven from the original 1930s garden – the American red, mulberry tree and Japanese maple. The Woodland Garden has an incredible array of colour when in bloom – with snowdrops, bluebells, crocuses and narcissus. There is also a stream replete with fish and a garden pond, where you'll find any number of birds, including ducks and the four resident flamingos.

Taken over by Virgin and often used for luxury entertaining the gardens are still open to the public for free (but do phone ahead before visiting, as the space is often booked for a private function). The gardens are now Grade II listed by English Heritage.

Also part of the garden complex is a popular and rather exclusive restaurant that has some stunning views of the skyline, and a private club often used for some of London's premier social events. Though not exactly kid friendly, they are a great example of London's VIP nightlife, to take in as you walk past with your pram and head home for an early night.

Royal Air Force Museum

Graham Park Way, Colindale, Barnet, London, NW9 5LL

WEB:	www.rafmuseum.org/london
TEL:	+44 (0) 208205 2266
EMAIL:	london@rafmuseum.org
COST:	free to enter, simulators and cinema are extra
OPENING TIMES:	10.00am–6.00pm daily (last entry 5.30pm)
AGE RANGE:	4+
BABY CARE:	change facilities at the toilets in each hall
FOOD:	restaurant, cafe, and plenty of picnic space
NEAREST STATION:	Colindale (Northern line), the museum is a 10-minute walk

In outer London, the Royal Air Force Museum is a child-friendly museum dedicated to the history of that service. With more than 100 aircraft on display and a 3D aviation cinema, the museum is sure to thrill any junior pilots in the family.

The vast museum is spread across a series of hangars – each with a different theme.

The most popular with children is usually the Aeronauts hangar. This interactive space allows kids to take the controls of a helicopter, try their skills at hang-gliding, as well as explore many exhibits demonstrating how flight works. Also popular with the kids is the 4D Theatre, where 3D animation combined with dynamic seating allows visitors to experience a range of missions. From a dogfight in the First World War, to racing through ravines at supersonic speeds, the excitement of piloting your own jet through the skies is brought to life for everyone in their seats.

Additionally there are two flight simulators at the museum – the Black Hawk Simulator in the Milestones of Flight hangar and the Historic Simulator in the Historic hangar. Both offer a selection of flight simulations: a flight with the Red Arrows, a low flying mission on a Tornado Jet… and more. There is a minimum height requirement of 1.2m for both simulators.

The Milestones of Flight hangar exhibits the major events in aviation history: the earliest planes ever built, the Wright brothers' first flight, Second

World War aircraft, and today's contemporary jet engines. It also has an interesting exhibit on Air Traffic Control.

Other hangars include: the Battle of Britain Hall, which documents this epic battle exhibiting aircraft, artwork, a sound and light show; the Bomber Hall, which tells the story of the bomber aircraft from the First World War to today; and the Marine Craft Collection, which exhibits some of the marine craft that have played a vital part in the RAF missions across the last 100 years – carrying equipment, aircrew sea survival exercises, and offering assistance to accidents at sea.

There are so many aircraft on display it is almost impossible to see them all. For those looking for something in particular, the website has a handy search function where visitors can locate any aircraft and find which hangar it is located in. The website also has a range of downloadable trails and quizzes for the various hangars, to help kids find their way around.

The museum sometimes has special events listed so check the website for things that are happening during your visit.

Science Museum

Exhibition Road, London, SW7 2DD

WEB: www.sciencemuseum.org.uk
TEL: +44 (0) 870 870 4848
EMAIL: feedback@nmsi.ac.uk
COST: free (there is a charge for some special exhibitions)
OPENING TIMES: 10.00am–6.00pm daily (last entry 5.15pm)
AGE RANGE: all ages
BABY CARE: change facilities on every level and a family room on the basement level
FOOD: several cafes, 2 picnic areas
NEAREST STATION: South Kensington (Piccadilly and District and Circle lines)

One of the most popular technology museums in Europe, the Science Museum in London is a wonder of science and exploration. From space travel and simulators to interactive experiments, there is something for all ages and all interests.

Spread across seven floors, the museum is divided into manageable chunks, each with its own theme. The Ground Floor holds the Exploring Space display, with two real space rockets hanging above your head, a section on satellites, and a full-sized replica of the 'Eagle' that landed on the moon in 1969. There is also an IMAX theatre on the ground floor and the Legend of Apollo 4D cinema (note, there is an entrance fee for both).

The First Floor includes Cosmos and Culture that traces the planet's history, and an interactive display that investigates genetics called *Who Am I?* Head to the Third Floor for the *Fly Zone* where you can experience a Red Arrows jet in the flight simulator, or take the controls and fly a jet yourself in the fly 360°. This floor is also where you will find the *Launchpad* area – a fabulous hands-on area for kids aged 8–14, to experience the world of physics and learn about how things work. Here kids can get their hands dirty, splitting light beams, examining the density of liquids and many more interactive experiments. *Launchpad* also regularly has shows and

science demonstrations for kids to get involved in. There is also a fabulous hands-on area for inquisitive 3-6 year olds called *The Garden*. Here, kids can explore key scientific areas – construction, water, light and sound – in a fun and multi-sensory space.

The Science Museum regularly has different exhibitions and galleries open so it is well worth visiting their website before you go to check out what is happening. They have a great 'plan your visit' section where you can find out everything that is happening on a particular day; you can also buy tickets online for any special exhibitions ahead of time to ensure you don't miss out.

The museum gets busy, especially on weekends, rainy days and during school holidays. However, with the Natural History Museum just around the corner, you can swap between the two, dependent on the queues at the front gates.

Somerset House

The Strand, London, WC2R 1LA

WEB:	www.somersethouse.org.uk
TEL:	+44 (0) 20 7845 4600
EMAIL:	info@somersethouse.org.uk
COST:	free to enter, exhibitions, workshops and special events are extra
OPENING TIMES:	Fountain Court: 7.30am–11.00pm
	Embankment level: 10.00am–6.00pm
	River Terrace: 8.0am–11.00pm
FOOD:	8 cafes and restaurants
AGE RANGE:	all ages
BABY CARE:	baby change facilities in the accessible toilets
NEAREST STATION:	Temple (District and Circle lines)

Somerset House is a stunning, neo-classical building, with a large courtyard and impressive architecture, and it has been used as the location for several Hollywood films – including *Golden Eye, Sherlock Homes,* and *Love Actually.*

As well as its spectacular design, Somerset House is also a centre for the visual arts and hosts some of best creative arts exhibitions and events in the city. The House is home to the Royal Academy, the Government Art School, the Courtauld Institute of Art and the Courtauld Gallery – which has a fine collection of impressionist paintings on display. There are also many other excellent galleries inside, such as the Embankment Galleries, that all have a range of exhibitions on display (see website for more details on what is on during your visit). There are many free public displays alongside the paid displays. The Visitors Centre has a display on the history of the building, as well as a café overlooking the river.

For families, Somerset House offers a great variety of family workshops, where families can take part in a range of creative arts activities together – model making, fashion design, painting... and more. Each session is designed to encourage creativity, so the workshops are a great opportunity for the whole family to get hands-on and do something a little different.

In the winter, the courtyard turns into a popular magical open-air ice rink, while in summer, the courtyard is filled with 55 floodlit dancing water fountains that are always a hit with the kids. The courtyard also hosts many open-air concerts, films, displays and events. See website for more details on what is appearing during your visit.

Tate Modern

Bankside, London, SE1 9TG

WEB:	www.tate.org.uk/visit/tate-modern
TEL:	+44 (0) 20 7887 8888
EMAIL:	visiting.modern@tate.org.uk
COST:	free to enter, exhibitions, workshops and special events are extra
OPENING TIMES:	10.00am–6.00pm Sun–Thurs, 10.00am–10.00pm, Fri–Sat
FOOD:	Tate Café on level 1 (sometimes run a kids eat free offer), 2 kiosks at the entrance, espresso bar on level 3, restaurant on level 6
AGE RANGE:	all ages, plus a dedicated Under 5 area
BABY CARE:	baby change facilities on site plus cloakrooms with buggy parking
NEAREST STATION:	Southwark (Jubilee line), Blackfriars (District and Circle line)

A modern art gallery might not typically be top of the list for parents to visit with children. But the Tate Modern has turned that impression on its head, creating a family-friendly museum with interactive art for all ages. By letting the children take the lead, often parents see art from a different perspective too!

There are always different artworks on display at the Tate – from sculpture and installations to photography and textiles, so check the website to see what is exhibiting during your stay.

As well as the exhibited art, on Level 3 you'll find the Bloomberg Connects Drawing Bar. Here, you can interact with digital projects, create a masterpiece and instantly see it displayed. The Drawing Bar also has a Flickr page of recent drawings.

There is an Interactive Zone on level 4 that has a range of interactive games and multimedia displays to encourage creativity and illustrate art through the ages.

For the youngest ones, on the 5th floor is the Under 5s Zone. With a musical slide, a mirrored house and many other sensory displays, it is the perfect space for toddlers to explore. There are also touch screens in this space for the slightly older ones.

The gallery offers a free art trail for kids that guides them through the artworks on display. There are also multimedia guides available that offer additional information on the art that is on display, as well as interviews with the artists.

© Tate Photography

As well as the everyday displays, the Tate Modern holds Open Studio sessions every weekend (11.00am–6.00pm). Here is an opportunity for all ages to play, experiment with different materials and ideas. Topics and media vary from season to season – from weaving, sculpture, textiles and construction – so check the website for more details.

The Tate Café sometimes has a 'kids eat free' menu (when accompanied by an adult meal), check the website if it is in place during your visit.

For art activities after your visit, the Tate Modern also has a fabulous interactive website for kids – kids.tate.org.uk – where you can send in your artwork, see other work, play art-based games, a wonderful resource for inspiration and creativity.

Once you are finished at the Tate, right outside is the Millennium Footbridge – the dramatic steel suspension bridge built in celebration of the millennium that spans the river to St Pauls Cathedral.

Can we play now?

London's best parks and playgrounds

London is one of the greenest cities in the world, with more than 3,000 parks or gardens to choose from. From the manicured gardens of Kensington Palace to the vast space of Richmond Park, there is an abundance of space for children to run and play freely. Visit in the summer and you'll find refreshment kiosks open for drinks and ice creams, and a bounty of wildlife to explore. London parks offer a fantastic assortment of play space too: adventure playgrounds, sensory trails, animal encounters... and more.

Alexandra Park

Alexandra Palace Way, London, N22 7AY

WEB:	www.alexandrapalace.com
TEL:	+44 (0) 20 8365 2121
COST:	free, activities are extra
OPENING TIMES:	9.30am–5.30pm (some activities vary, see listings or check website)
AGE RANGE:	all ages
BABY CARE:	change facilities available in accessible toilets
FOOD:	2 cafés and a pub
NEAREST STATION:	Wood Green (Piccadilly line), and catch the W3 bus

With panoramic views of London that stretch from Canary Wharf to The Shard, Alexandra Park is 196 acres of woodland, grassland, formal gardens and attractions. Known as the 'People's Park', it is a lovely park to simply wander around and get some fresh air, as well as being full of activities to keep the whole family entertained.

Most popular with the older kids is the pitch and putt course. Open from 10.00am to dusk, there are 10 holes to play. There is also a skate park for those wishing to challenge themselves on the ramps. For the younger kids to let off steam there is the Little Dinosaurs soft play centre. Open all year around from 9.30am to 5.30pm, it is a bespoke adventure soft play space, payable by the hour (kids under 1 are free). There is also a café nearby for refreshments.

For the whole family, pedal boats are available for hire on the boating lake from April to November. Also by the lake you'll find the Lakeside Café with free Wi-Fi, baby change facilities, colouring sheets for the kids and a yummy menu.

Alexandra Park has a small deer enclosure that is home to a herd of fallow deer. These deer are the direct descendants of the herd that lived here when the park was first designed. They are quite tame and happy to graze on the vegetation as they watch the visitors go by (but please don't feed the deer). Also in the park is a lovely ornamental rose garden to explore, plenty of open grassland and lots of shade for a picnic.

For a traditional English pub lunch, head to the Bar & Kitchen in the Victorian Palace, where they serve delicious homemade food daily and roasts on a Sunday. Open from 11.00am to 11.00pm, there is a fabulous outdoor terrace with spectacular views that is perfect for the kids to be noisy without a worry.

The main attraction of Alexandra Palace for many Londoners is the Ice Rink, offering ice-skating all year-round. Ice skating lessons are available and there is also a café inside.

Alexandra Palace is used for major events and concerts, and is often open to the public. Check the website for things happening during your visit. The park is also used for outdoor events, all which are always listed on the website.

Battersea Park

Battersea Park, London, SW11 4NJ

WEB:	www.batterseapark.org
TEL:	+44 (0) 20 8871 7530
COST:	free
OPENING TIMES:	8am–dusk
AGE RANGE:	all ages
BABY CARE:	change facilities in the accessible toilets inside the park
FOOD:	2 cafés; 2 snack bars; in summer there is always an ice-cream van within easy reach
NEAREST STATION:	Battersea Park (Overground line)

Battersea Park is just a short hop from Victoria, on the southern bank of the River Thames. Though Battersea is known for the rather monolithic power station (incidentally, now being transformed into exclusive apartments), the park next door is often regarded as one of London's most interesting, thanks to its wide variety of flora and fauna.

At 200 acres, the park is home to a large lake, all weather sports facilities including football pitches, tennis courts and a running track, reclaimed marshland and Battersea Park Children's Zoo (see page 10 for more details). An area of three hectares has been designated as a nature reserve, which is now home to an impressive range of woodland birds, as well as butterflies and the rare stag beetle.

Steeped in history, the park originated as a popular place for duelling. Officially opened as a park and public space in 1858, the park became home to local football team Wanderers FC, and it was here that the first football game under the Football Association Rules was played, on 9 January 1864. The park was also used to house anti-aircraft guns and several air-raid shelters during both world wars.

Nowadays, the park is one of tranquility and nature. There is plenty of birdlife to discover here, with herons, cormorants and grebes often feeding alongside the ducks around the lake. During July and August (and into September, weather permitting) you can rent a boat or pedalo to take out on the lake.

Battersea Park also has several beautifully landscaped historic gardens to explore, each with its own unique theme: the serenity of the Old English Garden, the impressive landscaping of the Russell Page Garden, and the exotic habitat of the Sub Tropical Garden. Battersea Park also boasts some of London's finest trees – some of them quite rare. In particular, the park is home to the beautiful hybrid strawberry tree – which is

the largest of its kind in Britain and probably dates back to the 1850s – and the holm oak, which was planted around 1863.

There are two playgrounds for the kids. For the under 5s, there is the Children's Playground with plenty of play equipment for the little ones to explore. Next to it is the Adventure Playground, designed for 5 to 16 year olds it has a climbing wall, rope swing, wooden walkways and a zip-line. There is also a nice picnic area inside.

Coram's Fields

93 Guildford Street, London, WC1N 1DN

WEB:	www.coramsfields.org
TEL:	+44 (0)20 7837 6138
COST:	free
OPENING TIMES:	09.00am–dusk
AGE RANGE:	0–16
BABY CARE:	children's toilets and baby-change facilities in the park
FOOD:	Pistachios in the Park
NEAREST STATION:	Russell Square (Piccadilly line)

Coram's Fields is one of London's gems, right in the heart of the city. A unique seven-acre (28,000 sqm) park and playground, it is also one of the most historically significant, being on the site of London's first home for abandoned children. Completely fenced, and with only one gate, it is the perfect place to let kids run free for a few hours. Adults are only allowed into the park when accompanying a child, and similarly, children cannot enter or leave without an adult, keeping the park very family-focused and safe.

The playground is well equipped for all ages, with several climbing frames, two large sandpits, and swings. There is also an adventure playground with aerial slide at the back of the park.

In the middle of Coram's Fields is a paddling pool that is open during the summer, which always proves hugely popular with kids of all ages, so take a change of clothes on a hot day.

With plenty of grassed areas, Coram's Fields is an ideal space for free play, or to relax under the trees. It is also a great spot for a picnic if you are in the area. If you haven't packed a lunch, the café Pistachios in the Park (open from March to October) serves food in the central buildings. There you'll find a healthy child-friendly menu including drinks and snacks as well as plenty of indoor and outdoor seating.

Coram's Field's is also home to a small city farm. Here kids can get up close with a range of farm animals – goats, chickens, rabbits and birds. If you are looking for special activities for the kids, the Children's Centre, in the middle of the park has a fantastic programme of events for various ages – including dance, art, soft play and sports. Check the website for details. Note, no dogs or bikes are allowed in the park.

Diana, Princess of Wales Memorial Playground

Broad Walk, Kensington Gardens, W2 2UH

WEB:	www.royalparks.org.uk/parks/kensington-gardens
TEL:	+44 (0) 300 061 2001
EMAIL:	dianaplayground@royalparks.gsi.gov.uk
COST:	free
OPENING TIMES:	10.00am–15.45/19.45
	(closing time is dependent on season, check website for details)
AGE RANGE:	0–12
BABY CARE:	change facilities in the accessible toilets at the entrance to the park
FOOD:	Refreshment stand
NEAREST STATION:	Queensway (Central line)

Known to most locals as the 'Pirate Ship Park', Diana, Princess of Wales Memorial Park is a wonderland of pretend and imaginative play, and one at which you can easily spend a whole afternoon.

Located in Kensington Gardens, the playground is designed around a theme of Peter Pan. Kensington Gardens was the inspiration behind the creation of the well-known children's story written by J.M. Barrie in 1902, and the Peter Pan theme is consequently dotted throughout the gardens.

The Princess of Wales Playground is huge, but is cleverly divided into manageable areas that are linked together with tunnels, secret pathways, and bridges. The biggest challenge for parents will be keeping up with the little ones!

At the centre of the playground is a fabulous pirate ship for kids to explore as well as a climbing frame with bridges and slides. Kids will also find teepees, 'tree phones' and delightful sculptures hidden throughout the lush backdrop. Designed for disabled kids to play alongside the able-bodied, the park also has a sensory trail, a musical garden, and the whole park is wheelchair and pram friendly. For the smaller kids, there is a sandpit, swings, a water fountain, and plenty of toddler-friendly play equipment.

In an effort to keep kids safe, adults can only enter if supervising a child, and children can only leave with an adult carer. There is also a capacity limit; so on sunny days, or on the weekend, there can be a queue to get in.

Being situated in Kensington Gardens, there are plenty of other activities in the vicinity. Kensington Gardens themselves are lovely to stroll through. Kensington Palace is nearby (see page 22 for more details) and the landscaped Italian Gardens are a short walk away (but keep an eye on any toddlers as the fountain walls are very low and they could easily tumble in).

The magical Peter Pan statue can also be found near the playground. Commissioned, paid for and arranged by J.M. Barrie, the statue was installed overnight on 1 May 1912 and has become synonymous with the park.

Greenwich Park

Greenwich, London, SE10 8QY

WEB:	www.royalparks.org.uk/parks/greenwich-park
TEL:	+44 (0) 300 061 2380
EMAIL:	greenwich@royalparks.gsi.gov.uk
COST:	free
OPENING TIMES:	6.00am–6.00pm/8.00pm (closing time is dependent on season, check website for details)
AGE RANGE:	all ages
BABY CARE:	change facilities in the accessible toilets dotted throughout the park, and in the information centre in front of the maritime museum
FOOD:	3 cafés and a number of refreshment kiosks throughout the park
NEAREST STATION:	Cutty Sark (DLR), Greenwich (Overground line), or catch the riverboat from Westminster

As the oldest enclosed Royal Park in London, Greenwich Park is also the most historic. Enclosed in 1427, it incorporates areas dating back to Roman times, as well as being home to the Meridian Line, the Royal Observatory, and a spectacular herd of deer. If you are on a day trip visiting the other attractions in the area, such as the *Cutty Sark* (see page 14), or National Maritime Museum (see page 74), Greenwich Park is the ideal place to take a break for a few hours.

At 74 acres, the park is part of the Greenwich World Heritage Site. From the top of the hill in the middle of the park, there are spectacular views over the River Thames back toward the city. The Royal Observatory is also at the top of the hill, along with the Pavilion Café.

In the visitors centre, there is a great interactive display for kids to learn about the meridian line and the history of the local area. Near to the Tea House Café, there is a children's playground with climbing frames, a sandpit, a house and a slide. In the summer and school holidays puppet shows and workshops are offered to visitors. The Tea House Café has baby-change facilities, high chairs and a good selection of drinks and snacks.

At the south-eastern end of the park is the Wilderness Deer Park – home to a herd of 16 fallow and 14 red deer. To protect the deer, the area is enclosed, but there are paths threading through the woodland with special viewpoints from which you can watch the animals. The deer park is also a sanctuary to many other forms of wildlife – nesting birds, wood mice, bats and the endangered stag beetle. Also in the deer park is the Secret Garden Wildlife Centre. Here visitors can find information on the wildlife within the park. The classroom at the Wildlife Centre also has one-way glass, which allows the room to double as a hide – enabling visitors to view the deer without startling the animals.

If the kids are inspired by history, there is a site of Roman ruins near the junction of Bower Avenue and Great Cross Avenue. Believed to date back to AD 43, the site is thought to have been a Roman-Celtic temple.

Greenwich Park also offers several beautifully landscaped gardens to explore. In the north-eastern corner of the park, the Queen's Orchard is a wonderful example of historical gardening. With fruit trees dating back as far as the 1500s and two ponds, the orchard still grows fruit and vegetables today. Dating back to 1925, the Herbaceous Border is London's largest of its kind, and can be found at the front of the Queen's House. The Rose Garden is located at the eastern side of the park and is very popular during early and mid summer.

Hampstead Heath

London, NW5 1QR

WEB:	www.cityoflondon.gov.uk/hampsteadheath
TEL:	+44 (0) 20 7332 3322
EMAIL:	hampstead.heath@cityoflondon.gov.uk
COST:	free
OPENING TIMES:	always open
AGE RANGE:	all ages
BABY CARE:	change facilities in the accessible toilets dotted throughout the park
FOOD:	2 cafés on Hampstead Heath and one at Kenwood House
NEAREST STATION:	Hampstead Heath (Overground line), Golders Green (Northern line)

A favourite open space for many Londoners, Hampstead Heath is a massive 790 acres of ancient woodlands, magical meadows, nature trails, and vast open space. Located just 6½ km (4 miles) from Oxford Street, you couldn't be further away from the frenetic city life that is on its doorstep. Not just a park, it is akin to stepping into the countryside for the day, and from the top of Parliament Hill, one of the highest points in London, you are afforded some spectacular views back toward the city.

At the southern end of the park is the Parliament Hill Lido. Hampstead Heath is famous for open-air swimming, with the Ladies and Men's Ponds being the only life-guarded open-air swimming facilities in the UK that are open every day of the year. Families tend to head for the Lido Pool – a 60-metre unheated open-air swimming pool that was built in 1938 – where there is also a paddling pool for the under 5s.

You'll also find an adventure playground at Parliament Hill, designed especially for the older kids.

Hampstead Heath is rich in wildlife and nature; and is recognised as one of London's best wildlife reserves. There are more than 800 veteran trees, some being rare species such as the midland hawthorn. More than 180 species of birds have been recorded here, with rare breeds such as the lesser spotted woodpecker, the kingfisher, swallow, garden warbler and great crested grebe being sighted. Hampstead Heath also has 30 ponds and countless glades to explore, all of which are teeming with local wildlife.

At Kenworth House, at the northern area of the Heath you'll also find an open-air theatre and 112 acres of English-style gardens to explore.

Hampstead Heath has an abundance of nature trails that weave their way across the heath. It can get muddy and not all paths are pram friendly. It is a place to easily get

lost for the day, so if you set off wandering, do take a map with you. See the website for a number of mapped trails.

The northern-western end of the park meets the formal, beautifully landscaped gardens of Golders Hill Park. Here you'll find a children's play area as well as tennis courts, all-weather table tennis tables, a croquet lawn and a café. There are also some lovely water gardens to explore. Golders Hill Park is home to a small zoo and butterfly house; both are free to enter.

For something a little different, head for the Pergola and Hill Gardens, found where Golders Hill Park meets Hampstead Heath, at the A502. Kids will love to explore this remarkable example of historic grandeur and opulence. Built in 1906, the once extravagant elevated walkway with its elaborate façade of columns is now overgrown with vines and flowers, leaving an eerie piece of history amidst the gardens.

Holland Park

London, W8 6LU

WEB:	www.rbkc.gov.uk/leisureandlibraries/parksandgardens/yourlocalpark/hollandpark
TEL:	+44 (0) 20 7361 3000
COST:	free
OPENING TIMES:	7.30am until 30 minutes before dusk
AGE RANGE:	all ages
BABY CARE:	change facilities at the café
FOOD:	1 café
NEAREST STATION:	Holland Park (Central line), High Street Kensington (District and Circle lines)

Considered to be one of the more romantic and tranquil parks in London, Holland Park is situated in the affluent borough of Kensington and Chelsea. Spanning 22 acres, the park is split into two areas – the woodland area at the northern end, and the formal gardens and sports area toward the Kensington end. There is also a delightful and appealing café in the middle of the park.

The semi-wild, quite dense woodland is magical for kids to explore. Here you can really get up close with some of London's wildlife – squirrels, peacocks, and native birds; there is even a herd of wild pigs that live in the woods! The pigs were introduced to the park in 2010 to reduce the nettles and brambles that were growing in the woodland and to create a meadow area for wild flowers. There are also two enclosed cow paddocks for grazing British Longhorn cows, also introduced to the park to restore the wildlife meadow. There is an ecology centre that can provide a wealth of information on the woodland, as well as maps for nature trails, a wildlife club with holiday activities, and outdoor activity programmes for the kids.

In the middle of the park you'll find the remains of Holland House – a large 17th century mansion house that was bombed during the Second World War. Part of the house has been restored and is now a youth hostel, and the rest provides a magnificent backdrop for the open-air theatre held here every summer.

Further south there are plenty of sports facilities including a cricket pitch and tennis courts. There are three playgrounds in the park: one with a sandpit, an adventure playground with slides, a trampoline, zip wires and climbing equipment for the older ones, and a third natural play space where kids can climb on logs and build dens out of twigs. There is also a giant chessboard, which all ages love to make use of.

The formal gardens include a spectacular flower garden that is different on every

visit, and the beautifully serene Kyoto Garden. Here, there is a pond teeming with colourful fish, a waterfall and a bridge that spans the water. The Chamber of Commerce of Kyoto donated the Kyoto Garden to London in 1991. Perfect for a picnic or a place to take a break for a few hours, the Japanese-styled garden is truly a world away from the busy London streets that surround the park.

Hyde Park

London, W2 2UH

WEB:	www.royalparks.org.uk/parks/hyde-park
TEL:	+44 (0) 300 061 2000
COST:	Free
OPENING TIMES:	5.00am–midnight
AGE RANGE:	all ages
BABY CARE:	change facilities located in accessible toilets dotted throughout the park
FOOD:	2 cafés, several refreshment points located throughout the park
NEAREST STATION:	Hyde Park Corner (Piccadilly line), Marble Arch (Central line), Knightsbridge (Piccadilly line)

Spanning more than 350 acres in the heart of central London, Hyde Park is one of London's most famous, and best loved parks. Here you can ride horses, hire bikes, take a stroll along one of the many paths that skirt the lake, or get lost amid the meadows, gardens and 4,000 trees. In the summer there are deck chairs for hire, ideal for sitting and watching the squirrels skip by.

In the middle of the park is the Serpentine lake, where you'll see swans, geese, ducks and other waterfowl. Boats and pedalos are available for hire: there is no charge for children under 4, but children under the age of 12 months are not permitted. Here you can also take a ride on the UK's first solar-powered boat – the Solarshuttle.

Also on the banks of the Serpentine is the Lido, which has a sun terrace, a children's play area and paddling pool as well as open water swimming. The Lido Café, on the waterside is a perfect place to stop for a bite to eat; watching the swans glide by as you tuck into your lunch. The water's edge is fenced, so no need to worry about the kids toppling in, however, there isn't much shade so do take sunscreen on a hot day.

For the older kids, there is an adventure playground on the southern edge of Hyde Park that has climbing frames, a slide and swings as well as plenty of space for free play.

One of the big attractions in Hyde Park is the Diana Memorial Fountain. Designed to reflect Diana's life and qualities – the water flows from a high point, swirling and bubbling to settle in a tranquil pool. There are three bridges to cross the water and reach the heart of the fountain, and visitors are welcome to sit on the fountain edge, dip their feet in and rest. It is not permitted to walk or stand in the water due to the stone being very slippery. The fountain area is gated and supervised when open (hours are 10.00am–4.00pm/8.00pm; closing time is dependent on the season, check website for details).

Hyde Park is where you will find Speakers Corner, the place where public speaking and debate has had a voice since the 1800s. Many famous orators such as George Orwell, Lenin, and Karl Marx have spoken here, as well as being the site for many suffragette meetings. Today, anyone can stand and express their views on a subject of their choosing.

Kew Gardens

Royal Botanic Gardens, Kew, Richmond, Surrey, London, TW9 3AB

WEB: www.kew.org
TEL: +44 (0) 20 8332 5655
COST: adults £11, children under 16 are free
OPENING TIMES: 9.30am until 5:00pm/7.30pm
(closing time dependent on season, check website for details)
AGE RANGE: all ages
BABY CARE: baby-change facilities at Victoria Gate and the cafés within the park; whole park is pram friendly
FOOD: 4 cafés and restaurants within the grounds: White Peaks café is family-friendly with healthy choices, a dedicated kid's food display and plenty of indoor and outdoor seating
NEAREST STATION: Kew Gardens (District and Overground lines)

On the outskirts of London, Kew Gardens is a one of the world's most famous gardens. Boasting over 100 kid-friendly attractions, an incredible array of plants and more than 14,000 trees it is the ideal place to learn about nature and plant-life of England, and somewhere you can easily spend a day exploring.

Kew is home to several glasshouses, each with their own purpose. The Waterlily House is an enchanting space and home both the world's largest and smallest water lilies. For something more diverse, the Princess of Wales Conservatory has 10 zones, each a different climate, one of which has an area for carnivorous plants that is always a hit with the kids. Other houses include the Palm House – one of the largest surviving Victorian glasshouses in the world and home to the Marine Aquarium – and the Alpine House, home to the fragile plants of mountainous regions.

Kew Gardens is home to Britain's first interactive botanical play zone. Designed to inspire an interest in botany among younger visitors, Climbers and Creepers offers a fabulous play space where

kids can climb inside a plant to learn about pollination, interact with giant carnivorous plants, and more.

Just outside the Climber and Creepers space, Treehouse Towers is a tree-themed play area designed for 3–11 year olds. There is plenty of equipment to keep the busiest of climbers happy, with scramble nets, slides, rock-climbing walls, rope bridges and towers to explore.

For the over 7s, the Log Trail is a play space where the older kids (and adults!) can climb and balance on a natural play area constructed of fallen trees (make sure everyone has sturdy footwear for this one).

For those interested in English wildlife, head to the Wildlife Observation Centre. Here you'll find a human-sized badger set, where you can discover how badgers live, via a network of 1–1.5 metre/3-5 feet high tunnels that connect nests, food stores and sleeping areas. Kew is home to around 24 badgers; they are a protected species here.

Stretching over 300 acres, the Arboretum at Kew contains some of the area's oldest trees, some dating back to 1759 – when the gardens were first opened. Above the Arboretum, you'll find the Tree Top Walkway. The 18-metre high (59-feet) walkway takes visitors through the upper branches of some of the most spectacular trees, to see birds, insects, seed pods and to explore life among the canopy. Prams are not allowed on the walkway, and there are 118 steps to access its start.

Regent's Park

London, NW1 4NR

WEB:	www.royalparks.gsi.gov.uk
TEL:	+44 (0) 300 061 2300
COST:	free
OPENING TIMES:	5.00am–4.00pm/7.00pm
	(closing time dependent on season, check website for details)
AGE RANGE:	all ages
BABY CARE:	change facilities located in accessible toilets dotted throughout the park
FOOD:	6 cafés in the park as well as many refreshment kiosks
NEAREST STATION:	Regent's Park (Bakerloo line), Camden Town (Northern line), Baker Street (Bakerloo, Jubilee, Circle, Metropolitan, and Hammersmith lines)

At 410 acres, Regent's Park is a large open parkland – the largest grassed area for sports in Central London. It is also home to London Zoo (see page 32), an open-air theatre that hosts performances from May to September, and numerous other outdoor activities.

The space began as a hunting park for Henry VIII, was later leased as farmland, and by the early 19th century architect John Nash had planned for a series of grand townhouses and a summer palace to be built on the space. The plans proved unprofitable and later that century the park was opened to the public. Few elements of Nash's original design remain, though the outer circle he planned forms the boundary of the park today, now edged with grand townhouses.

Regent's Park boasts a wealth of wildlife. With a large lake, many islands, the Regent's Canal (see page 82) and countless mature trees, the park is a sanctuary for its many feathered residents. A pair of peregrine falcons have nested on a building on the outskirts of the park since 2003, the Heronry on the boating lake is home to more than 20 pairs of nesting herons, and the lake itself is home to more than 650

waterfowl including ducks, swans and geese. You may also see hedgehogs (nocturnal), grey squirrels and wood mice scurrying amid the undergrowth.

For those with a love for wildlife, the Wildlife Garden is well worth visiting: it was designed to demonstrate how to encourage wildlife in your own back garden. There is artwork from local children incorporated into the walkways and information boards.

Queen Mary's Gardens, in the middle of the inner circle and near the open-air theatre, is where you'll find London's largest collection of roses. The gardens are best visited in June, when the flowers are in full bloom. The Avenue Gardens, at the southern end of the Broad Walk also offer a stunning example of formal gardens. Centred around a large stone bowl known as the Lion Vase, the tiered gardens fan out, with Victorian-style planting as well as restored ornaments filled with flowers and immaculate hedging.

For those with a need to be active, boats and pedalos can be hired on the boating lake (from 10.00am–6.00pm). There are also kid-size boats available on weekends for the over 5s.

Outdoor sports are a key part of Regent's Park with cricket and football pitches, netball and tennis courts, a running track and a 'trim trail', soon to be upgraded. There are four playgrounds in Regent's Park. The best are at Hanover Gate, on the west side of the Park and near the boating lake, where you'll find two play areas – a timber adventure playground for the older ones with a sandpit, and an easy access space for the younger ones.

As you head out of Regent's Park, to the north is Primrose Hill. At 63 metres (more than 200 ft) above sea level, the view from the top is spectacular.

Richmond Park

London, TW10 5HS

WEB:	www.royalparks.gsi.gov.uk
TEL:	+44 (0)300 061 2200
COST:	free
OPENING TIMES:	pedestrian gates open 24 hours a day, except during the deer cull in November and February, when the gates are open 7.30am–8.00pm. Vehicle gates open 7.00am–dusk
AGE RANGE:	all ages
BABY CARE:	change facilities located in accessible toilets at the main gates
FOOD:	2 cafés in the park as well as many refreshment kiosks
NEAREST STATION:	Richmond (Overground and District lines)

To the south west of central London is Richmond Park – the largest of the Royal parks. Spanning 2,500 acres, it is most famous for being home to more than 650 red and fallow deer.

The deer are a large part of the park's history, and they have roamed here since 1529. The young are born in May to July, so watch for fawns among the undergrowth. Does are sensitive and protective of their young during this time, so take care not to disturb them. Autumn is when you'll see the bucks, or the male of the species 'rut' – an impressive display of clashing antlers performed to attract female attention and deter rivals. During Autumn, the park is particularly stunning, as the tree line becomes an array of golds, reds and oranges as the leaves turn.

For the plant-lovers, the Isabella Plantation (open all year round) is a haven of exotic and ornamental gardens and woodland to explore. Because of its organic habitat, the Isabella Plantation is a particularly good place to see birdlife, such as the tawny owl, woodpecker, sparrow hawk and bullfinch.

The landscaped ornamental gardens at Penbroke Lodge are also wonderful to explore. The lodge has a lovely terrace and tea room overlooking the gardens that serves sandwiches, snacks and kids' lunchboxes.

Outdoor activities are everywhere in

Greawolf © The Royal Parks

Giles Barnard © The Royal Parks

Richmond Park. One of the best ways to get around this vast space is to hire bikes from the parkcycle centre, which is located near Roehampton Gate. For the more adventurous, horse riding is a popular way to explore the park (visit www.ridinginlondon.com), while for anyone looking for an adrenalin kick, Richmond Park is the place to try the increasingly popular sport of power kiting (visit www.kitevibe.com).

In the north-west corner of the park, King Henry's Mound provides spectacular views of the city and the Thames Valley. The steep mound was originally thought to be the location where Henry VIII stood when a rocket was fired from the Tower of London to signify the execution of his wife Anne Boleyn for treason. However, this has since been proved unlikely.

There are two playgrounds in Richmond Park. The Kingston Gate Playground is ideal for the under 5s, with timber play sculptures to climb, multi-use equipment, a bark pit, and a children's picnic area. For older kids there is the Petersham Gate Playground, with a sandpit, climbing frame with jumping lily pads and balancing blocks, water play and a giant xylophone.

Richmond Park can get muddy and not all paths are paved, so not everywhere is pram-friendly.

St James's Park

London, SW1A 2BJ

WEB:	www.royalparks.org.uk/parks/st-jamess-park
TEL:	+44 (0)300 061 2350
EMAIL:	stjames@royalparksgsi.gov.uk
COST:	free
OPENING TIMES:	05.00am–midnight, every day
AGE RANGE:	all ages
BABY CARE:	change facilities located in accessible toilets dotted throughout the park
FOOD:	4 refreshment kiosks within the park, or for something special try Inn the Park café
NEAREST STATION:	St James's Park (District and Circle line), Westminster (Jubilee, District and Circle lines), Charing Cross Station (Northern, Bakerloo and British Rail lines)

With Buckingham Palace, St James's Palace and Horse Guards Parade on its doorstep, St James's Park is possibly London's most regal park. With The Mall running along one side, it is also the backdrop for many ceremonial parades that are held in the city, including the annual Trooping the Colour.

Once a swampy wasteland that was used for pigs to graze, the land was turned into a deer park by Henry VIII in 1536; the hunting lodge being where St James's Palace stands today. Today, St James's Park is a truly elegant park. It has a large lake in the middle, where you can see the famous pelicans, as well as owls, woodpeckers and many other beautiful birds. The pelicans are fed every day at around 2.30pm (check website for up-to-date times). At the eastern end of the lake is Duck Island – the nature reserve and breeding ground for swans, pelicans and other waterfowl. The park is also teeming with squirrels and other wildlife, so take your camera as many are tame and will stand still long enough for you to take a quick pic.

Spanning the centre of the lake is the Blue Bridge, which offers stunning views across the water to Buckingham Palace

and Big Ben. Whilst at the eastern end of the lake, is the spectacular water plume, titled Tiffany Fountain.

Being such a pleasant inner-city park, deck chairs are available for hire between March and October – which serve as a great way to relax and watch the world go by, if the kids (or you!) need a rest for a short while.

Once the kids have had enough of exploring the 13 monuments and statues in the Park, you'll find a usually not too overly crowded playground with a swing, slides, a sandpit at the eastern end.

If you want to soak up a traditional royal ceremony, the Changing the Guards happens between 11.00–11.30am every day during summer, and alternate days during the winter (visit www.royal.gov.uk for up-to-date times).

Kids love to see the soldiers with their large bearskin hats marching down the grand, tree-lined avenue. In the summer this does get busy, so be prepared to get there early and stand around if you want a spot near the front; it is less busy and just as good a vantage point along The Mall.

I'm hungry...
Child-friendly eateries

Eating out with kids can sometimes spark a certain amount of dread in many parents, and hearing those words 'I'm hungry' can quickly spin you into a panic. Thankfully, London is well equipped with kid-friendly cafes and pint-sized healthy portions... all within easy reach.

KEY:

££££	–£10 for a main
££££	£11–15 for a main
££££	£16–20 for a main
££££	£21+ for a main

Chains and city-wide

Today there are plenty of restaurant chains that offer fabulous healthy alternatives to the old-fashioned fast food options. From organic breakfasts to wraps and salads, they are family friendly and have menus to keep both kids and adults happy.

ASK Italian

WEB: www.askitalian.co.uk
TEL: +44 (0)845 602 2704
PRICE: ££££

ASK Italian has 11 restaurants across London, all serving fresh authentic Italian food: pizza, pasta, risotto, meat, fish and salads, as well as takeaway pizza. The kids' menu has a choice of pizza, pasta, and all kids meals can be made with gluten-free pasta or dough.

Café Rouge

WEB: www.caferouge.co.uk
PRICE: ££££

French-inspired bistro chain Café Rouge has 23 restaurants in London open daily for breakfast, lunch and dinner, and everything in between. From patisseries and baguettes, to steaks and mussels, the menu is simply huge. The children's menu is also quite extensive, with most fussy eating challenges covered.

EAT

WEB: www.eat.co.uk
PRICE: ££££

Great for an easy and healthy breakfast and lunch, there are about 80 EATs dotted across the city. Reasonably priced, most have space to sit in, but you can also take-away. Menus change daily, dependent on the season; everything is made fresh from scratch. Breakfasts include toast, porridge, cereals, pastries and yoghurts. Lunch includes sandwiches, soups, pies, salads, hot rolls and hot pots. With a focus on working toward a sustainable future, EAT is quite active within the local community, tackling food waste and poverty.

Giraffe

WEB: www.giraffe.net
PRICE: £££

There are 13 Giraffe restaurants across London, with freshly cooked food, music and a lively atmosphere. Open for breakfast, lunch and dinner, it is noisy, friendly, relaxed and very child-friendly. The kids' menu is huge, with plenty of healthy and fussy-eating options; the main menu is an eclectic mix of burgers, Mexican, grills, stir-fries, pastas and salads. They often have meal deals on, so check the website for up-to-date details.

Leon

WEB: www.leonrestaurants.co.uk
PRICE: ££££

With a slogan of 'naturally fast food' you know that Leon will be a hit with everyone in the family. Served in lunchboxes and snack pots it still feels a bit like fast food, so the kids are satisfied, yet the food is healthy, nutritious and delicious. They have a huge range of simple breakfast and lunch options: poached eggs and beans, bacon and egg muffin, meatballs, grills, salads, soup, burgers, and plenty of healthy snacks and sides. There is a children's menu too that will suit the tiniest and fussiest of tummies.

Nando's

WEB: www.nandos.co.uk
PRICE: £fff

Always popular with kids, you'll find Nando's restaurants scattered throughout London. It's not fast food, as everything is cooked to order, but it's not a fancy restaurant either… a combination that works well for families. With a menu based on Portuguese-style chicken, they serve burgers, wraps and a range of sides. Perfect for fussy eaters, you can personalise everything – from how spicy to have the chicken, to fillings and style of bread. They have some healthy sides such as salads, peas, beans, coleslaw and corn on the cob, as well as the regular chips, mash, rice and garlic bread. They have a dedicated children's menu with small portions and frozen yogurt desserts. There is a fun pack available with games to play and finger puppets to make; there are even crayons on the tables. All restaurants have highchairs and most have baby-change facilities.

Pizza Express

WEB: www.pizzaexpress.com
TEL: +44 (0)20 7563 7723
PRICE: ££ff

Often thought of by Londoners as the best pizzas in town, the Pizza Express chain is ever growing, with currently more than 30 restaurants across the central London area. Pizza Express serves traditional Italian-style pizzas, with quality ingredients and a unique mix of toppings – keeping the adults happy as well as the children. They have a number of gluten-free choices as well as a fabulous healthy options range. Their affordable kids' menu includes a starter, choice of pasta, pizza (including a make-you-own option), sorbet, ice cream and a bambinocchino. Tables can be booked ahead on the website.

Pret A Manger

WEB: www.Pret.com
TEL: +44 (0)20 7827 8000
PRICE: £fff

A staple food for any Londoner, you'll find a Pret A Manger cafe in nearly every retail stretch in London. With shelves full of healthy ready-made sandwiches, snacks, drinks and fruit, it is a great choice for parents on the go. Everything is freshly made on-site using natural, preservative-free ingredients, and the contents are clearly labeled for any fussy eaters. Even better, they serve organic coffee and have a solid sustainability policy, with produce sourced locally. Most have space to eat in, but otherwise it provides great picnic food for a lunch in the park.

Spaghetti House

WEB: www.spaghettihouse.co.uk
TEL: +44 (0)20 7395 0390
PRICE: ££££

With pizza and pasta being such a family staple, it's no surprise that Spaghetti House is a popular choice for families. There are 12 restaurants across central London, all serving a huge range of traditional Italian pasta, pizza, seasonal dishes, salads and sides. They offer a two-and three-course children's menu with a good selection of meals. During peak tourist season it can get very busy, but you can book a table on the website.

Wagamama

WEB: www.wagamama.com
No phone
PRICE: ££££

Known the world over for their ramen-style bars, there are several Wagamama restaurants in central London. With share tables and bench seats, the fun and vibrant setting make it a popular choice for families. Serving a huge range of Japanese-inspired dishes, there is something for everyone: teppanyaki, curries, salads, ramen, noodles, to name a few. They also have a substantial children's menu with smaller portions, healthy choices, and ice-lolly desserts.

   If the kids can't sit still and you prefer to head to the park, Wagamama also has a take-away option.

Wahaca

WEB: www.wahaca.co.uk
PRICE: ££££

This Mexican mini-chain has 14 restaurants across central London serving tasty Mexican-inspired dishes throughout the day: tacos, taquitos, quesadillas, as well as steaks, salads and fish. They also have a kids' menu with smaller portions and fewer spices, as well as a kids 'build your own' taco menu. The restaurants are always bustling, so there's no need to worry about the kids making noise. Wahaca is focused on sustainability and sourcing ingredients ethically.

Of course, one of the handiest options for dining out with kids in London is the traditional English pub. Wherever you turn in London, there is usually a good pub within easy reach. Most pubs have now realised that being child-friendly is essential, offering kid-sized portions and a more relaxed environment, including outdoor seating where kids can be less restrained. Many also have menus to colour in and play equipment in the garden.

Most have a board outside the front entrance with meals of the day. Look for a children's menu of combined meal deals. Food in chain pubs tends to be cheap, but for really good homemade meals, head for the independent pubs that now form a growing trend of gastro pubs. A beer garden is a winner; any outdoor seating on a sunny day can be the perfect antidote to cranky-hungry children, rather than trying to sit still in an enclosed restaurant. Though not always the healthiest choice, pub food is usually lovely and simple, making it an easy staple for kids – with chips, sausages, pies, pasta and burgers, as well as a good range of 'grown up' food.

Children aren't allowed in a bar area, so the pub needs to have a designated dining space or an outdoor space. Some of the best local pubs are listed in the local sections to follow.

Eateries by area

Whether you are in the vibrant west end or the tree-lined suburbs, child-friendly restaurants in London are never too far away; you can often find a real local gem tucked down a side-street. With an abundance of cuisines to suit even the fussiest of eaters, you may even tempt your children to try something new!

Central London

All Star Lanes
Victoria House, Bloomsbury Place, London, WC1B 4DA

WEB: www.allstarlanes.co.uk/venues/holborn
TEL: +44 (0)207 7025 2676
EMAIL: holborn@allstarlanes.co.uk
COST: ££££

If the kids are feeling particularly rambunctious, at All Star Lanes you can combine dinner with a game of ten pin bowling. A good selection of burgers, fish, ribs and nibbles are on both the main menu and kids' menu, and special meal deals are available.

Belgos
50 Earlham Street, Covent Garden, London, WC2H 9HP

WEB: www.belgo-restaurants.co.uk
TEL: +44 (0)20 7813 2233
COST: ££££

Huge, bustling and fun Belgian restaurant, serving mussels, frites, burgers, rotisserie chicken, steaks, and their popular signature dishes. They have a separate kids' menu with smaller portions of pasta, fish, sausages and chicken. Free Wi-Fi and express lunch deals available.

Bella Italia

22 Leicester Square, London, WC2H 7LE

WEB: www.bellaitalia.co.uk
TEL: +44 (0)20 7321 0016
COST: £££

Next door to the Odeon Leicester Square, this vibrant Italian restaurant serves pizza, pasta and grills. Open for breakfast, lunch and dinner, and for occasional celebrity watching. It has a good children's menu.

Bodean's BBQ Soho

10 Poland St, London, W1F 8PZ

WEB: www.bodeansbbw.com
TEL: +44 (0)20 7287 7575
EMAIL: soho@bodeansbbq.com
COST: £££

A menu stacked with ribs, chicken wings, burgers, salads, steaks and a huge selection of sides that guarantees that nobody will go hungry. Plus, pick up a loyalty card and kids can eat free during the day. All restaurants have highchairs and baby-change facilities. There are a couple of other Bodean's restaurants in London – in Fulham, Clapham, Tower Hill and Balham – but Soho is the most popular.

Byron

24–28 Charing Cross Road, London, WC2H 0HX

WEB: www.byronhamburgers.com
TEL: +44 (0)20 7240 3550
COST: £££

Serving 'proper' hamburgers, the way burgers used to be made with a choice of toppings and sauces. Byron also has a kids' menu with mini burgers and macaroni cheese.

Fields Bar & Kitchen

Lincoln's Inn Fields, London, WC2A 3LH

WEB: www.fieldsbarandkitchen.com
TEL: +44 (0)20 7242 5351
EMAIL: fieldsbarandkitchen@benugo.com
COST: ££££

In the middle of the park, Fields Bar & Kitchen serves all day sandwiches, pasta, soup, salads and pizzas. With a huge outdoor terrace, and space for the kids to play on the grass, it is perfect for a relaxed family lunch.

Five Guys

5–6 Argyll St, London, S1F 7TE

WEB: www.fiveguys.co.uk
TEL: +44 (0)20 7434 3407
COST: ££££

A popular US chain, Five Guys is a build your own burger outlet with 250,000 possible combinations. Voted as #1 Burger in Washingtonian Magazine's 'Readers Choice' since 1999 it can get busy, but everyone says it is worth it.

Homeslice

13 Neal's Yard, Seven Dials, London, WC2H 9DP

WEB: www.homeslicepizza.co.uk
TEL: +44 (0)20 7836 4604
EMAIL: info@homeslicepizza.co.uk
COST: £££££

Delicious woodfired pizza cooked in an open oven and served whole; kids can slice and serve their own pizza (though watch their little fingers!). 50/50 ordering is welcome, for those that can't agree on toppings. It is nice and busy, so it's not a place where you need to worry about being quiet.

Hix Soho

66–70 Brewer Street, London, W1F 9YP

WEB: www.hixsoho.co.uk
TEL: +44 (0)20 7292 3518
COST: ££££

Bring along your budding artists to Hix Soho Kids Art and Food Club. Kids can draw a picture of their experience at HIX for a chance to win a free meal, a couple of cocktails for Mum and Dad, and a signed cook book (competition drawn at the end of every month). The menu is fabulous – a signature blend of seasonal British food – on both the main and the kids' menu.

Inn The Park

St James's Park, London, SW1A 2BJ

WEB: www.peytonandbyrne.co.uk
TEL: +44 (0)20 7451 9999
COST: ££££

Inn the Park serves gourmet cuisine in a picturesque setting, on the bank of the lake in St James's Park. They have a great kids' menu, with colouring and puzzles, outdoor seating and plenty of space nearby for a run-around.

Lanes of London
140 Park Lane, London, W1K 7AA

WEB: www.lanesoflondon.co.uk
TEL: +44 (0)20 7647 5664
EMAIL: book@lanesoflondon.co.uk
COST: ££££

In one of London's most famous streets, Lanes of London offers a mix of British and international dishes via a menu of delicious small plates, mains and desserts. It has a superb kids' menu including mini beef burgers, breaded fish, warm chocolate muffins and hand-crafted cupcakes. The quintessential afternoon tea is now possible... even with the kids! Open for breakfast, lunch, afternoon tea and dinner.

Masala Zone
48 Floral Street, London, WC2E 9DA

WEB: www.masalazone.com
TEL: +44 (0)20 7379 0101
EMAIL: coventgarden@masalazone.com
COST: ££££

Priding itself on providing some of London's best informal Indian dining, Masala Zone has a great selection of curries, dahls, street food and breads. They have a great kids' menu with fussy-eating options. There are also restaurants in Bayswater, Camden Town, Earls Court, Islington and Soho; each one visually unique – Covent Garden is a favourite with several hundred puppets suspended from the ceiling.

Porters English Restaurant

17 Henrietta Street, Covent Garden, London, WC2E 8QH

TEL: +44 (0)20 7836 6466
EMAIL: neil@porters.uk.com
COST: ££££

World famous pies, fish and chips, and classic British dishes Porters English Restaurant is a great choice for the family. The kids' menu contains a selection of the grown-up food, just in smaller portions.

Rainforest Café

20 Shaftsbury Ave, London, W1D 7EU

W: www.therainforestcafe.co.uk
T: +44 (0)20 7434 3111
COST: ££££
E: customercare@therainforestcare.co.uk

Rainforest Café is a jungle-themed, kid-friendly restaurant, with waterfalls, moving animatronics and a rainforest-themed menu with lots of kid-friendly and healthy options. Very popular so is worth booking.

Shake Shack

Covent Garden, 24 Market Building, The Piazza, London, WC2E 8RD

WEB: www.shakeshack.com
TEL: +44 (0)1923 555129
EMAIL: info@thewellshampstead.co.uk
COST: £££££

Shake Shack serves gourmet burgers, hot dogs, shakes and fries, all freshly prepared with no artificial ingredients. Gluten free options available.

Serpentine Bar & Kitchen

Serpentine Road, Hyde Park, London, W2 2UH

WEB: www.serpentinebarandkitchen.com
TEL: +44 (0)20 7706 8114
EMAIL: serpentine@benugo.com
COST: ££££

Located in the middle of Hyde Park, on the edge of the Serpentine Lake, the Bar & Kitchen serves pizzas, sandwiches, salads and mains. Kids' menu also available. There is plenty of outdoor seating and space for the kids to play.

The Riding House Café

43–51 Great Titchfield St, London, W1W 7PQ

WEB: www.ridinghousecafe.co.uk
TEL: +44 (0)20 7927 0840
EMAIL: info@ridinghousecafe.co.uk
COST: ££££

Eclectic brasserie tucked just behind Oxford Street serving locally sourced British cooking – breakfast, lunch and dinner. No separate kids' menu, but plenty of choices for fussy eaters.

Tom's Kitchen

Somerset House, Strand, London, WC2R 1LA

WEB: www.tomskitchen.co.uk
TEL: +44 (0)20 7845 4646
EMAIL: tomskitchen@somersethouse.org.uk
COST: ££££

Though more upmarket than some, Tom's Kitchen is still very workable with kids. Fabulous chef, preparing a good choice of British favourites with a twist. Open for brunch, lunch and dinner.

Trafalgar Square Café

Trafalgar Square, WC2N 5DN

WEB: www.cafeonthesquare.co.uk
COST: ££££

In the heart of one of London's most iconic locations, the Trafalgar Square Café is open daily, serving sandwiches, cakes, drinks… and provides the perfect backdrop for a morning coffee.

Vingt Quatre

111A Great Russell Street, London, WC1B, 3NQ

WEB: www.vq24hours.com
TEL: +44 (0)20 7736 5888
COST: ££££

Open 24 hours a day, this is the ideal spot for any parents with early risers. Serving all-day breakfasts, great fry-ups, burgers, pasta, and salads, it's buzzing yet relaxed. They have a kids' menu with small portions and fussy-friendly options.

North

Bill's
9 White Lion Street, London, N1 9PD

WEB: www.bills-website.co.uk
TEL: +44 (0)20 7713 7272
EMAIL: islington@bills-email.co.uk
COST: ££££

Open for breakfast, lunch, dinner and everything in between, this is a buzzing café with a substantial menu of burgers, salads, grills, pies and delicious desserts. The kids' menu caters for all tastes with pancakes, eggs and beans for breakfast, or sausages, ribs, pasta, burgers and macaroni cheese for mains.

Carluccio's
32 Rosslyn Hill, London, NW3 1NH

WEB: www.carluccios.com
TEL: +44 (0)20 7794 2184
COST: ££££

A superior Italian restaurant serving fresh, authentic Italian cuisine. Kids' menu includes a lovely selection of the main menu but in smaller portions. Carluccio restaurants are now popping up all over London.

Honest Burgers
Unit 34a, Camden Lock Place, London, NW1 8AF

WEB: www.honestburgers.co.uk
TEL: +44 (0)20 8617 3949
COST: ££££

Using locally sourced ingredients, Honest Burgers focus on serving simple burgers and doing it well. They have a kids' menu for smaller portions and unique side dishes such as sweetcorn and cauliflower fritters. They also have branches in Soho, Portobello Market, Kings Cross, Oxford Circus and Liverpool Street.

Lakeside Café
Alexandra Palace, London, N22 7AY

WEB: www.alexandrapalace.com
TEL: +44 (0)20 8365 2121
EMAIL: info@lakesidecafe.co.uk
COST: £££££

On the edge of the lake at Alexandra Palace, this café is perfect for a casual bite to eat. Simple café food – snacks, light meals – and plenty of activities nearby to keep the kids entertained.

Pavilion Café (N10)
Highgate Woods, London, N10 3JN

TEL: +44 (0)20 8444 4777
COST: £££££

A quaint café on the edge of Highgate Wood, with a picket fence, outdoor terrace, and playground nearby. A comprehensive menu is on offer that includes snacks and drinks, sandwiches, pasta and mains; the menu often changes.

The Clissold Arms
115 Fortis Green, Finchley, London, N2 9HR

WEB: www.clissoldarms.co.uk
TEL: +44 (0)20 8444 4224
EMAIL: info@clissoldarms.co.uk
COST: ££££

Voted best family pub in London, The Clissold Arms is a family-orientated gastro pub with good quality British dishes with European influences. Fabulous garden for the kids, often with a bouncy castle and community activities. For the parents, the Clissold Arms is also the home of The Kinks and there is a room dedicated to memorabilia. Traditional roasts are served on a Sunday. Baby-change room available.

The Fish & Chip Shop

189 Upper Street, London, N1 1RQ

WEB: www.thefishandchipshop.uk.com
TEL: (0)20 3227 0979
COST: ££££

A 'posh' fish and chip shop, with all the traditional food you'd expect as well as a good selection of seafood extras. Kids' menu includes shrimps, hot dog, fish and chips, and some yummy desserts. The menu also doubles as a colouring and puzzle sheet.

The Highbury Barn

26 Higbury Park, Angel & Islington, London, N5 2AB

WEB: www.thehighburybarnpub.co.uk
TEL: +44 (0)20 7226 2383
EMAIL: Highbury.Barn@greenwich-village-inns.com
COST: ££££

Open for breakfast, lunch and dinner, serving traditional homemade food and Sunday roasts. An iconic and child-friendly pub, but avoid when Arsenal are playing at home as it can get very busy before a match. No separate kids' menu but portions are ample to share. There is plenty of space for prams and baby-change facilities too.

The Narrow Boat Pub
119 St Peters Street, Islington, London, N1 8PZ

WEB: www.thenarrowboatpub.com
TEL: +44 (0)20 7400 6003
EMAIL: narrowboat@youngs.co.uk
COST: ££££

A true gem, the Narrow Boat Pub is on the Regent's Canal. It serves traditional pub fare for lunch and dinner and delicious roasts on a Sunday. It has a good children's menu that has traditional roasts in pint-sized portions on a Sunday.

The Wells Pub
30 Wells Walk, London, NW3 1BX

WEB: www.thewellshampstead.co.uk
TEL: +44 (0)20 7794 3785
EMAIL: info@thewellshampstead.co.uk
COST: ££££

A lovely gastro pub with a delicious menu and cracking Sunday roasts. Children's menu available.

South

Café on the Rye
Strakers Road, Peckham Rye Common, London, SE15 3UA

WEB: www.cafeontherye.co.uk
TEL: +44 (0)20 8693 9431
EMAIL: Fiona@cafeontherye.co.uk
COST: ££££

A place where the whole family is sure to find something to enjoy eating, the menu has everything from continental breakfasts, sandwiches, salads and daily specials, to a kids' menu of pasta, beans on toast, simple sandwiches, sausages and eggs. Being in the middle of the Common, there is plenty of space for the kids to play (which will hopefully give you enough chance to drink your coffee).

Cubana

48 Lower Marsh, London SE1 7RG

WEB: www.cubana.co.uk
TEL: +44 (0) 7928 8778
EMAIL: reservations@cubana.co.uk
COST: ££££

Cubana offers a Latin American and Cuban-inspired menu with a mouthwatering range of tapas, mains and delicious cocktails. Kids' menu contains a healthy selection including falafel, chicken bites as well as fruit smoothie and homemade desserts. They also have a cheaper street food lunch menu. All ingredients are 100 per cent free range.

Eco

62 Clapham High Street, London, SW4 7UG

WEB: www.ecorestaurants.com
TEL: +44 (0)20 7978 1108
EMAIL: eco@ecorestaurants.com
COST: ££££

A local institution, Eco has been making delicious and affordable pizzas for more than 20 years. It is a family-friendly place with free Wi-Fi. Baby-change facilities are available. They have a separate kids' menu with little portions of starters, pizza, pasta, deserts and drinks. Also open for breakfast at the weekend.

Fish!

Cathedral Street, Borough Market, London, SE1 9AL

WEB: www.fishkitchen.co.uk
TEL: +44 (0)20 7407 3803
EMAIL: info@fishkitchen.com
COST: ££££

Family-friendly restaurant serving a huge choice of fresh seafood – cooked to order. Open for lunch and dinner, as well as breakfast and brunch at the weekend. Has a popular outdoor terrace; kids very welcome.

Pavilion Café (SE21)

Dulwich Park, off College Road, London, SE21 7BQ

WEB: www.pavilioncafedulwich.co.uk
TEL: +44 (0)20 8299 1383
COST: ££££

Hugely popular with parents, this picturesque family café is surrounded by green space for the kids to play. Food is freshly cooked to order; a traditional blend of café-style foods – breakfasts, soups, sandwiches and a kids' menu. Gluten-free, vegetarian and vegan options available.

The Garrison Public House

99–101 Bermondsey St, London, SE1 3XB

WEB: www.thegarrison.co.uk
TEL: +44 (0)20 7089 9355
EMAIL: info@thegarrison.co.uk
COST: £££

The Garrison Public House is a family-friendly restaurant open for breakfast, lunch and dinner. Nice atmosphere and interesting menu of British food with a twist. No separate kids' menu, but plenty on the menu to keep everyone happy.

The Manor Arms

Mitcham Lane, London, SW16 6LQ

WEB: www.themanorarms.com
TEL: +44 (0)20 3195 6888
EMAIL: manager@themanorarms.com
COST: £££

The Manor Arms is a wonderfully unpretentious local pub serving all-day sandwiches, burgers, pizzas and specials. Gluten free options available. No kids' menu but portions are hearty enough to share. Nice beer garden for the kids to be noisy in without worry.

The Rosendale

65 Rosendale Road, West Dulwich, London, SE21 8EZ

WEB: www.therosedale.co.uk
TEL: +44 (0)20 8761 9008
EMAIL: info@therosedale.co.uk
COST: ££££

The Rosendale is a fabulous pub serving traditional, simple and sustainable British food. They have a great garden that includes a climbing frame and table tennis for the kids; table football and boules for adults. Kids' menu available all day that includes pizza, fish fingers, burgers, sausages and roasts on a Sunday.

The Table Café

83 Southwark Street, London, SE1 0HX

WEB: www.thetablecafe.com
TEL: +44 (0)20 7401 2760
EMAIL: shaun@thetablecafe.com
COST: ££££

Relaxed all-day dining on the Southbank, serving yummy breakfasts, sandwiches, burgers, salads, famous waffles, and award-winning brunch.

East

Cantina Del Ponte
36c Shad Thames, London, SE1 2YE

WEB: www.cantinadelponte.co.uk
TEL: +44 (0)20 7403 5403
EMAIL: cangtina@dandlondon.com
COST: ££££

Family-friendly Italian with outdoor seating and spectacular views of The Thames. Serving 2- and 3-course set menus for lunch and dinner, as well as a la carte options. Basic kids' menu; kids can garnish their own pizzas.

Pavilion Café (E9)
Crown Gate West, Victoria Park, E9 7DE

TEL: +44 (0)20 8980 0030
EMAIL: info@the-pavilion-café.com
COST: ££££

Busy café in the heart of Victoria Park, open for breakfast, lunch and snacks. Has outdoor seating with plenty of space for the kids to run around.

Rivington Grill
178 Greenwich High Road, London, SE10 8NN

WEB: www.rivingtongreenwich.co.uk
TEL: +44 (0)20 8293 9270
COST: ££££

Perfectly located for a nice meal after visiting the various attractions in Greenwich, Rivington Grill is a buzzing restaurant serving simple British dishes. Open for breakfast, lunch and dinner. Kids eat free during the day from a kids' menu that includes fish and chips, burgers, chicken, and bangers and mash.

Springfield Park Café
Off Upper Clapton Road, Clapton, London, E5 9EF

WEB: www.springfieldparkcafe.co.uk
EMAIL: info@springfieldparkcafe.co.uk
COST: £££££

A child-friendly café serving fresh, seasonal and nutritious food from around the world: breakfasts, salads, soups, paninis, and hot meals. There is also a good selection of snacks, cakes and drinks. Picturesque setting in the park with plenty of space to play, the garden is fenced to avoid little guests wandering off.

Tom's Kitchen
11 Westferry Circus, London, E14 4HD

WEB: www.tomskitchen.co.uk
TEL: +44 (0)20 3011 1555
EMAIL: canarywharf@tomskitchen.co.uk
COST: £££££

One of the most child-friendly spots in town, this kitchen has a fabulous play room for the kids, a tasty kids' menu – for both breakfast and lunch – and if that's not enough, kids eat free from 10.00am–4.00pm on weekends. For the grown ups, there is a delicious menu of traditional food with a modern twist – such as steak, schnitzel, fish pie, and pork belly.

Tramshed
32 Rivington Street, London, EC2A 3LX

WEB: www.chickenandsteak.co.uk
TEL: +44 (0)20 7749 0478
EMAIL: reservations@tramshedshoreditch.co.uk
COST: £££££

Tramshed has a simple menu of steak and chicken to share, open for brunch, lunch and dinner. Kids' menu with mini steak, chicken burger, steak burger and spaghetti with tomato sauce. Even better, kids eat for free from 12.00pm–6.00pm.

Unity Kitchen Café

1a Honour Lea Avenue, Queen Elizabeth Olympic Park, E20 1DY

WEB: www.unitykitchen.co.uk
TEL: +44 (0)20 7241 9076
EMAIL: goodtimes@unitykitchen.co.uk
COST: ££££

Located next to Tumbling Bay adventure playground, this family-friendly café serves fresh and healthy café-style food. Activity sheets are provided to keep kids entertained.

West

Daylesford Organic Farmshop

208–212 Westbourne Grove, Notting Hill, London, W11 2RH

WEB: www.daylesford.com
TEL: +44 (0)20 7313 8050
EMAIL: manuel.pasqui@daylesford.com
COST: ££££

Organic farm shop and café open all day for breakfast, lunch, afternoon tea and dinner. Menus are seasonal, including full breakfasts, soup, burgers, salads, fish, pulled pork, and cheese platters.

Fait Maison Tea House

Ravenscourt Park, Paddenswick Road, London, W6 0UL

WEB: www.fait-maison.co.uk
TEL: +44 (0)20 8563 9291
EMAIL: info@fait-maison.co.uk
COST: ££££

Open 8.00am–5.00pm, serving freshly made salads, healthy children's meals, cakes and ice cream. There is an enclosed outdoor play area; kids' yoga classes are held outside during the summer.

Julies

135 Portland Road, London, W11 4LW

WEB: www.juliesrestaurant.com
TEL: +44 (0)20 7229 8331
EMAIL: info@juliesrestaurant.com
COST: £££

The ultimate in child-friendly dining, Julie's restaurant even runs a supervised crèche on Sunday afternoons for kids to play in once they finish their meal (check website for opening times), so you can finish lunch at your own pace. Great menu and it has plenty of kid-friendly healthy choices.

Poppy's Place

255 Munster Road, London, SW6 6BW

WEB: www.poppysplacesw6.co.uk
TEL: +44 (0) 20 7920 6420
EMAIL: hello@poppysplacesw6.co.uk
COST: £££££

Serving yummy all-day breakfasts, salads, sandwiches, burgers and soup, Poppy's place is a favourite spot for brunch for many locals. Kids' menu is great, with eggs, beans and fruit for breakfast; fish fingers, chicken, sausages and pasta for lunch. In the evening it turns into a lovely little candlelit restaurant.

Sticky Fingers Restaurant

1A Phillimore Gardens, London, W8 7QB

WEB: www.stickyfingers.co.uk
TEL: +44 (0)20 7938 5338
EMAIL: bookings@stickyfingers.co.uk
COST: £££££

Created by Rolling Stones' legend Bill Wyman, Sticky Fingers is his idea of what a good restaurant should be. Really kid-friendly, with a great kids' menu of ribs, chicken legs, burger, sausage or fish bites; it's a place both kids and adults can enjoy.

The Belvedere

Off Abbotsbury Road, Holland Park, London, W8 6LU

WEB: www.belvedererestaurant.co.uk
TEL: +44 (0)20 7602 1238
COST: ££££

If you feel like an upmarket lunch, the Belvedere is a good child-friendly choice. Staff are friendly, the kids' menu is delish, and the restaurant is bustling… so no need to worry about the kids being too noisy. Holland Park is also on the doorstep for a run around afterwards (see page 108).

The Golden Hind

73 Marylebone Lane, London, W1U 2PN

WEB: www.thegoldenhind.snack.ws
TEL: +44 (0)20 7486 3644
COST: £££££

Established in 1914, The Golden Hind serves West London's best fish and chips. No separate kids' menu but portions are large enough to share around.

The Victoria

10 West Temple Sheen, London, SW14 7RT

WEB: www.thevictoria.net
TEL: +44 (0)20 8876 4238
EMAIL: bookings@thevictoria.net
COST: £££££

Gastro-pub serving traditional comfort food and roasts on a Sunday. It has a dedicated kids' menu with the same traditional pub fare in little portions. With a large play area for the kids, The Victoria is a popular choice for families of south London.

Where are we going today?

Five family-friendly days in London

With so much to choose from and never enough time, a visit to London with kids can often feel overwhelming. To help ease the decision-making, here are five days out, planned to include many of the highlights as well as covering all the kid-friendly facts you need.

Day 1: Greenwich and East London

Starting at Westminster, catch the boat from Westminster pier down the river to Greenwich pier. There are several operators that run the same route (see page 162–167 for more information on transport). If you go with the River Tours or Thames River Services, you get a fabulously entertaining tour, with plenty of little facts about what you pass along the way.

When you arrive, take your choice of one or two of the Royal Museums Greenwich. There is the *Cutty Sark* (see page 14), the National Maritime Museum (see page 74) the Queen's House (see page 75) and the Observatory and Planetarium (see page 38). If you decide to visit more than one it is well worth combining your ticket purchases into the Big Ticket offer (see page 172).

After a busy morning at the museums, grab lunch from one of the many cafés in Greenwich Park (see page 104) or, on a nice day, find some shade for a picnic in the huge grassed area – there are a number of kiosks in the park selling sandwiches and snacks.

If the kids need a run-around, there is a great playground near the Tea House. Alternatively, if it is naptime take the pram for a stroll through the Deer Park for an escape into the wilderness.

After a break in the park, head into Greenwich and catch the DLR train and Jubilee line to North Greenwich. Here you can choose to spend the afternoon at the Emirates Aviation Experience (see page 16), which includes a return trip on the cable car and entrance into the Aviation Experience at the O2 or, if you prefer something with a view, take a single trip on the cable car over the river to Royal Victoria, and from here catch the Jubilee line to London Bridge to fit in a trip up the Tower Bridge Experience (see page 44) or the View from the Shard (see page 42).

For dinner there is a Pizza Express nearby on Borough High Street that has a kids' menu, high chairs and a very kid-friendly environment.

© National Maritime Museum, London

© The View from The Shard

Day 2: The South Bank

For the morning, book tickets in advance for a trip on the London Eye (see page 28). After taking in the views on Europe's largest Ferris wheel, head east along the Southbank, past Jubilee Gardens to Queen Elizabeth Hall to grab some lunch at Wahaca Southbank.

If the kids need a run around, head back to Jubilee gardens where there is a fantastic new playground with climbing equipment, grass areas and seating. If it is naptime and you need to take a walk with the pram, continue east along the Southbank where you'll pass street performers, markets and eventually reach Shakespeare's Globe – the rebuilt theatre that stands just a few hundred metres from its original site. If you are interested in the history, you can take a tour of the theatre, even take in a performance (if the kids will sit still for that long!).

The Millennium Bridge – that connects the Tate Modern (see page 92) to St Pauls – is nearby and well worth a wander over. This pedestrian steel suspension bridge was opened in June 2000 as part of the Millennium celebrations. Initially known as the 'wobbly bridge' (thanks to an engineering flaw that made the bridge wobble slightly when walked on), the problem was quickly fixed and is now an impressive piece of the river landscape.

If Shakespeare isn't your thing and you don't have a need to roll the pram for an hour, instead stick around Jubilee Gardens and book a tour of London on Duck Tours (see page 26). Once the tour is finished, head east along the Southbank and wander over the Waterloo Bridge (or you can always catch the tube from Waterloo to Temple if you like), and pop into Somerset House (see page 90) for a play in the fountains (summer) or ice rink (winter) and dinner.

© The London Eye

© London Duck Tours

Day 3: Kensington and the museums

Catch the tube over to South Kensington, and visit either the Science Museum (see page 88) or the Natural History Museum (see page 78), or both if you've got the stamina. They are right next door to one another, and both are treasure troves of entertainment for young and old. Both museums can get busy during school holidays, and the Natural History in particular can have large queues, so it's worth getting there early.

Both have picnic space inside the museums, as well as cafés, but if you've had your fill of the museums and fancy something a little different, pick up some sandwiches and take a walk up to High Street Kensington to have a picnic at The Roof Gardens Kensington (see page 84). Remember that it's worth phoning ahead to check availability, as the Roof Gardens are sometimes closed for private functions.

For a break and a run-around after lunch, head into Kensington Gardens where you'll find the fabulous Diana Memorial Playground (see page 102), as well as endless green space and gardens to explore. Look out for the Peter Pan statue nearby and the Round Pond where you can sail model boats. If it's a nice day, head to neighbouring Hyde Park (see page 110) where you can hire a pedalo, swim in the Serpentine lake, feed the swans or dip your feet in the Diana Memorial Fountain.

For dinner, wander back to High Street Kensington for some rock n roll ribs at Sticky Fingers (see page 146), or try a Giraffe Burger (see page 123) near Bond Street.

Day 4: Regents Park, London Zoo and North

Catch the tube to Regent's Park station and start the day with a walk through the magnificent Regent's Park (see page 114). Walk past the boating lake and see the Heronry, or through the Inner Circle to the open-air theatre and the impressively manicured Queen Mary's gardens. Stop at Hanover Gate for a run-around at the adventure playground, or hire pedalos on the boating lake. When you've had your fill of the park, continue on to London Zoo (see page 32), which can be found in the centre of Regent's Park. Here you'll see an incredible array of animals spread across 17 easy-to-navigate areas.

There is plenty of space for a picnic in London Zoo, as well as lots of café options. But if you want something a little different, exit the zoo and walk along the Regent's Canal (see page 82) to Camden Lock. Here you'll find a market space with an abundance of food options – from noodles and burgers to organic and vegan. Camden is a very colourful, bohemian part of London, and is great to wander around and take in the atmosphere for a while, if the kids oblige. The markets are rather maze-like, however, and not all areas are pram-friendly.

From here, head back toward the Baker Street area – either walking back through Regent's Park, or jump on the tube and catch the Northern line to Warren Street.

Nearby, on Marylebone Street, you can find Madame Tussauds famous waxworks museum, which is often popular with older kids. However, as this isn't always of interest to younger kids (unfortunately they don't understand who many of the celebrities are) the British Museum (see page 60) is just a short walk away at Russell Square. Also nearby is Coram's Fields (see page 100) for a run-around and play.

For dinner, head into Fitzrovia – the small group of streets that stretch between Tottenham Court Road, Oxford Circus and Goodge Street. On Charlotte Street you'll find a fabulous selection of restaurants, cafes and pubs, most of which have kids' menus and outdoor seating, and all have a fabulous 'London' vibe.

Day 5: West End, on a budget

Start the day at Trafalgar Square. Not only does it offer fabulous photo opportunities, kids always love to explore and climb on the many fountains and statues. Nearby there are several free museums to choose from. The National Gallery, on the northern side of Trafalgar Square offers family trails for all different ages, craft workshops during school holidays and weekends, and early years' sessions for the under 5s. The Portrait Gallery (see page 76), around the corner on St. Martin's Place is home to more than 200,000 portraits – from the 17th century to the present day – and also has family activities and free sketchpads to take around the museum.

Once you've had your fill of the museums, head over to Covent Garden for lunch. Here you'll find a myriad of eateries as well as plenty of prime space to watch the many street performers and eat a sandwich.

For something a little different in the afternoon, wander down Oxford Street to Oxford Circus and catch the Number 12 bus, which takes you along the picture-perfect tour of central London, without paying for a tour. It will take you along Regent Street, past Trafalgar Square and Piccadilly Circus, down Whitehall, past Westminster and Big Ben before crossing Westminster Bridge. Alight as soon as you have crossed the bridge at Lambeth North tube station and catch the tube back to Oxford Circus where, if you are brave enough, you can take the kids to possibly the most impressive toy shop in Europe – Hamleys on Regent Street. Otherwise, head down to Leicester Square where the buzz of London's west end is at its most vibrant.

There are plenty of options nearby for dinner: see pages 144–147 for some suggestions.

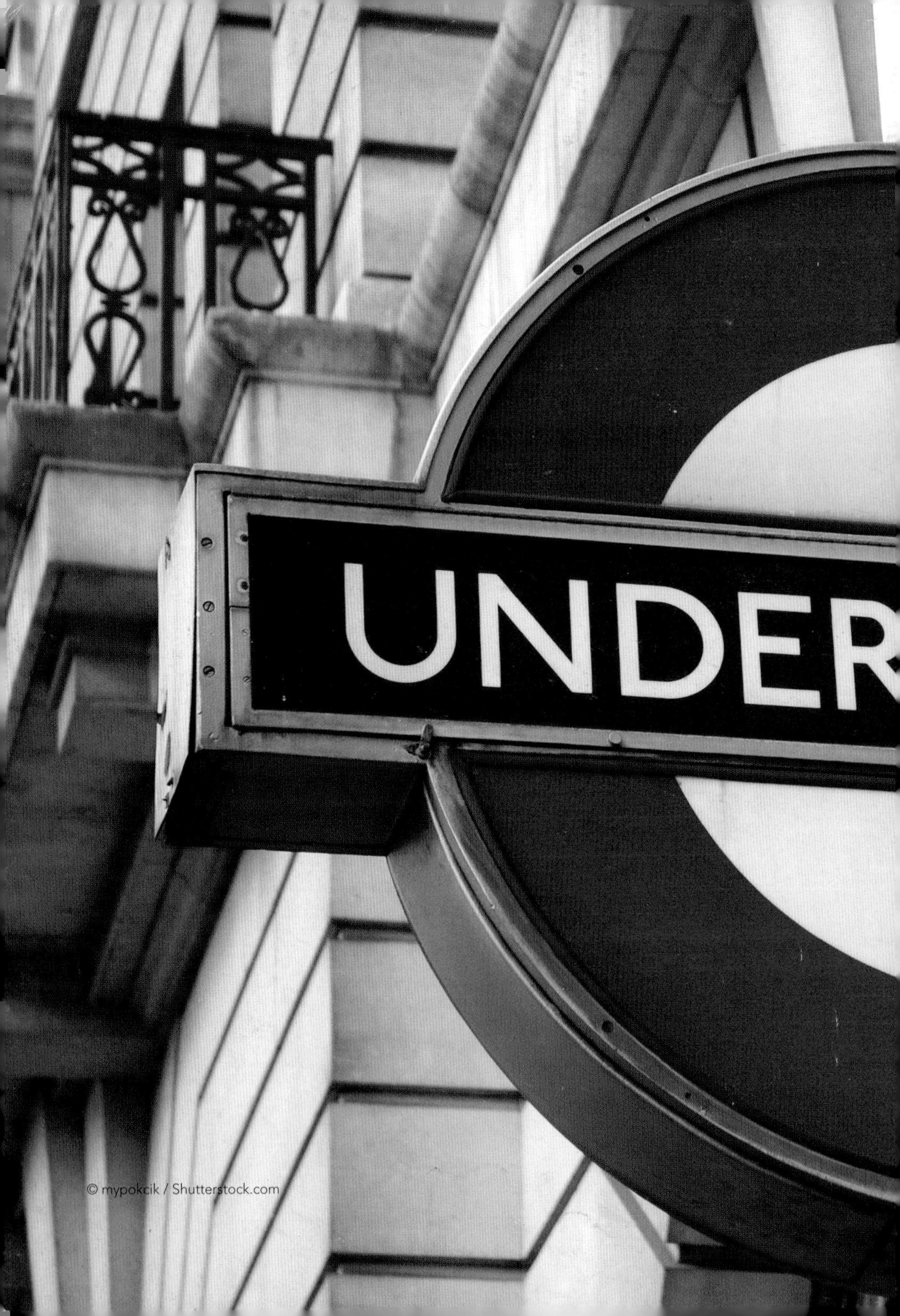
UNDER

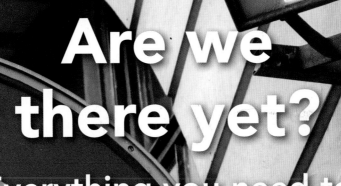

Are we there yet?

Everything you need to know for getting around

London has one of the most efficient public transport networks, providing visitors and locals with an affordable and quick way to get around the vast city. Though the journey might be a little more chaotic – with kids, a pram, and probably half the contents of your house along for the ride – navigating London's busy streets doesn't have to be arduous… it could even be fun!

Transport

Though one of the best ways to get around London is by foot, when you need to travel further than you're prepared to walk, there are various transport options within easy reach.

The London Underground

Known to most as 'the Tube', the London Underground is a fabulous way to get around. The trains and stations are clean, the exits and platforms are clearly signposted, and the trains run every few minutes between 5.00am and midnight.

First opening in 1863, the London Underground is considered to be the world's oldest rapid transport system. Steeped in history, many of the stations doubled as air raid shelters and part of the Central Line served as an underground fighter aircraft factory during the Second World War.

Today, there are 12 tube lines and a Light Rail that combine to efficiently cover the whole city. All lines are clearly labelled by name and colour (see map on page 164), so you can quickly and easily get to where you want to be.

With 3.5 million journeys made every day on the Tube, it can get very busy so try to avoid travelling at rush hour, if possible (in particular 7.00–9.00am and 4.00–6.30pm).

Not all stations have lifts and nearly all have escalators or stairs so if you are travelling with a pram, be prepared to do some carrying or bumping up and down the stairs. However, all the entrances do have wide ticket gates for prams. Transport for London (TFL) website – www.tfl.gov.uk/maps – has a step-free map so if you prefer to avoid those stations with stair access you can plan your journey accordingly. But if you don't need it, best to ditch the pram and go with a baby-carrier. The TFL website map section also has a great map showing which stations have toilets and baby-change facilities.

Tickets:
- Oyster Card
- Travelcards
- Single and return tickets
- Children under age 11 travel for free, if accompanied by an adult with a valid ticket

London buses

The iconic London double-decker bus is a very convenient and cheap way to get around London. Catching the bus also doubles as a great sightseeing opportunity: try routes 9, 12, 14, 15 and 22 to take in some of London's best sights.

Buses have been used as a form of transport in London since 1829, starting with a horse-drawn service that carried 22 people from Paddington to Bank. Motorised buses hit the streets in 1902 and since then, the bus network has grown to include a fleet of 8,765 buses in service today.

Transport for London (TfL) has a fabulous bus journey planner at www.tfl.gov.uk. Simply enter your current location, and where you want to get to, and it calculates the best route for you. The site also has maps of all the routes so you can follow your journey on a map. With all the buses fitted with GPS, TfL also offers a bus tracking service at www.countdown.tfl.gov.uk, so you can check when the next bus is due to arrive.

All buses on the network (apart from the rare, open-back heritage Routemaster bus) are low-floor vehicles, so can be accessed with a pram. However, at busy times it is better to collapse the pram and carry on board for space reasons.

Tickets:
- Oyster Card
- Travelcards
- You cannot pay cash on the bus
- Children under age 11 travel for free, if accompanied by an adult with a valid ticket

Overground trains

Linking up with the Tube network and the national rail network, the London Overground has four lines that skirt around central London and extend to the outer London areas. Trains don't run as often as the Tube, so it is worth checking schedules prior to travelling to avoid waiting around for too long.

Being part of the London transport system, the Overground is covered on the TfL website journey planner at www.tfl.gov.uk and the network is included on the map on page 164.

Tickets:
- Oyster Card
- Travelcards
- Children under age 11 travel for free, if accompanied by an adult with a valid ticket

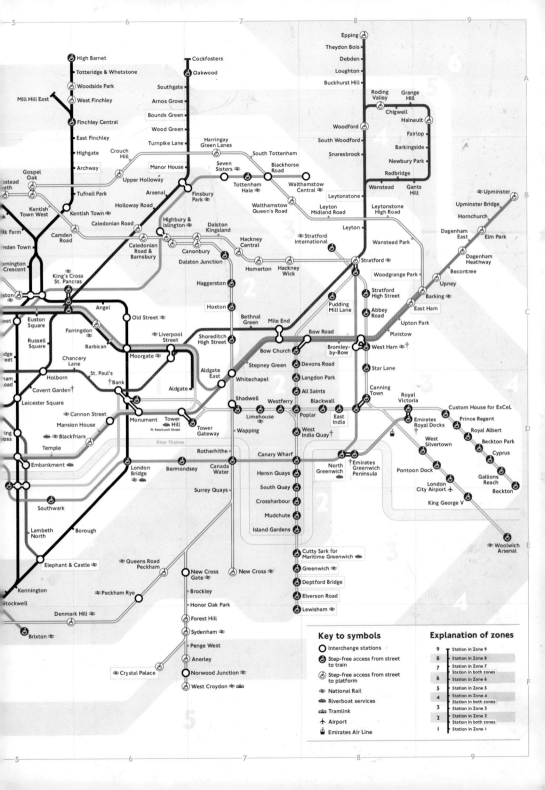

Black taxis

'Black cabs' are everywhere in London; their iconic design being an intrinsic part of the London landscape. If there is ever a time when you can't face trundling the family on public transport, a black cab is a great way to get from A to B.

To get their license, all black cab drivers must pass a driving test called 'The Knowledge' – a stringent taxi license test that has the reputation as the hardest to pass in the world. Described as 'like having an atlas of London imprinted on your brain', it apparently takes two to four years to learn all the routes. This means that whatever black cab you get into, simply name the landmark, hotel, point of interest or street name and the driver will know the shortest and fastest route to get you there... without the aid of satnav or other fancy gadgets.

Black cabs can be hailed on the street and can carry five people. A cab with a light in its front window is available for hire. A cab with a light out is spoken for. Prams can be taken in a cab without collapsing, so you don't need to worry about having a car seat.

Tickets:
- Cash or card in the cab

Ferries and riverboats

Beating the traffic and with fantastic views, London riverboats offer a fabulous and very family-friendly way to get around and experience the city. Most ferries have refreshments and Wi-Fi, and you are usually guaranteed a seat. All have accessible ramps and prams can be taken on board.

The fastest and cheapest option is to take the River Bus. Operated by MBNA Thames clippers, there are five River Bus services along the river, from Putney Pier to Woolwich. Timetables and a map can be found at www.tfl.gov.uk/maps/river. If you have a valid Oyster card or Travelcard you can get one-third off the standard fare. If you have an Oyster pay-as-you-go, you can get 10 per cent off the ticket price.

A more leisurely network is the River Tours service, which often have commentary and interesting facts along the way. Again, if you have a valid Oyster card or Travelcard you can get one-third off the standard fare; timetables and maps can be found at www.tfl.gov.uk/maps/river.

There are a number of other operators that have ferries along the Westminster to Greenwich route, one of the more popular is Thames River Services – see www.thames-riverservices.co.uk for tickets and times. If you have a valid Travelcard or Oyster card, discounts are available when booking at the ticket office.

Tickets:

- Oyster Card, but get one-third off the standard fare if you have present your Oyster card or Travelcard when booking
- Children under age 5 travel for free, if accompanied by an adult with a valid ticket

Emirates Air Line

Offering 360-degree views of London as you glide over the river, the Emirates Air Line is a cable car that links the north and south banks of the river – travelling from Greenwich Peninsula to the Royal Docks. The cars depart every 30 seconds and a one-way trip takes approximately 10 minutes.

This can be tied in with the Emirates Aviation Experience, see page 16 for more details.

Tickets:

- Travelcard, but receive a discounted fare if you present your Travelcard when booking
- Oyster pay-as-you-go
- Cash fares available at the ticket office
- Multi-journey tickets
- Children under age 5 travel for free, if accompanied by an adult with a valid ticket

London Cycle Hire

If you are travelling with older kids and everyone enjoys cycling, London has a fabulous bike-sharing scheme available. Known as the 'Boris Bike' (being named after Boris Johnson, who was mayor when the scheme was introduced), the bikes offer Londoners a cheap, easy and environmentally friendly way to get around the city. The bikes are especially useful for getting around the city parks and those areas of London where the streets are congested and easier to reach by foot (or by pedal).

Simply find a docking station at www.tfl.gov.uk/modes/cycling, use your credit card to hire the bike, and return the bike to any docking station within 24 hours. The website not only tells you where the docking stations are, but also how many bikes are available for hire, and how many spaces are available for returning. The first 30 minutes are free, after that it is £2 per ride. The website also has a number of maps to help you on your way, including cycle superhighways and leisure routes.

Tickets:

- You cannot pay with Oyster Card or Travelcards
- Pay by credit card

Tickets

There are a variety of ways to buy tickets for transport in London, each with their own benefits.

Standard Oyster Card: A plastic smartcard that holds credit for fares. You tap on and off as you pass through the ticket barriers. Buy at any tube station, top up online or at the touchscreen ticket machines at tube stations; you need one card per person. You can return the card at any Tube station once you are finished with it and your deposit is returned.

Visitor Oyster Card: Can be purchased online ahead of time and mailed to your home address, or you can purchase a two-day version when you arrive with unlimited travel in Zones 1 and 2. These cards are also sold in a number of overseas travel agents.

Contactless: Use a contactless debit or credit card to tap in and out on the yellow card reader to pay for your trip. Each person needs their own contactless card to travel; watch for the green light when you touch the card reader to make sure your card has been accepted. Be aware that if your card is from overseas, additional credit card charges could be applied. You can also use your contactless card to top up your Oyster Card at the ticket machines.

Travelcards: A paper ticket that allows you to travel as much as you like on the Tube, buses and overground trains. Can be purchased as 1-day or 7-day versions. Paper tickets are inserted at the ticket barriers.

Single tickets: Purchased at the ticket machine at tube stations, one per trip, they are used on the Tube, DLR, Overground and national rail services.

But Mummy said...

Useful information for your stay

Knowing where to go for the essentials is often something that can make or break a holiday with kids. Whether it's skipping a queue, an emergency toilet call, or fingers stuck in a toaster, being able to fix life's little problems is something all parents must be ever prepared for.

I have an ouchie

The main provider for health care in the UK is the National Health Service (NHS). For UK residents, all treatment on the NHS is free. Overseas nationals are only entitled to emergency treatment, so it is advisable to have travel insurance.

Emergency treatment can be found at any Accident and Emergency department of NHS hospitals. Central London hospitals include:

Charing Cross Hospital, W6 8RF
Chelsea and Westminster Hospital, SW10 9NH
King's College Hospital, Denmark Hill, SE5 9RS
Royal Free Hospital, NW3 2QG
The Royal London Hospital, E1 1BZ
St Mary's Hospital, W2 1NY
St Thomas', SE1 7EH
University College Hospital, NW1 2BU

For emergency services, call 999 (emergency line) or 111 (NHS medical advice line) or see www.nhs.uk to find your nearest A&E.

NHS walk-in centres are also available for minor and non-urgent cases and are dotted across London. Central London locations include:

Angel Medical Practice, N1 0DG
Guy's Hospital, SE1 9RT
Soho Square, W1D 3HZ
St Bartholomew's Hospital, EC1A 7BE
St Thomas', SE1 7EH
University College Hospital, NW1 2BU

Check www.nhs.uk for your nearest centre.

Most high street pharmacies are open from 9.00am to 6.00pm for medicines and non-urgent conditions.

I need a wee

Knowing the location of the nearest toilet – at all times – suddenly becomes an essential part of daily life once you are a parent. Being caught short can make the difference between 'making it' and getting on with your day, and 'not making it' and looking for the nearest bargain clothes store.

Luckily London is well equipped, with facilities usually located within an easy dash. All museums, department stores, galleries and public buildings have public toilets. All parks also have public toilets – usually marked on the signposts and maps at the gates. Some tube stations also have toilets, though they might require a silver coin at the turnstile. Most cafés, pubs, fast-food outlets and hotels will also allow you to use their facilities… especially if you have a cross-legged toddler holding your hand.

If toilets are at the very top of your crucials list (for example, if you are mid-training), www.greatbritishpublictoiletmap.rca.ac.uk is a brilliant website that will locate the nearest toilet to wherever you are.

But I'm not tired

London has accommodation to suit every budget and every size family. Most deals are found booking at least 3–4 months prior to your stay (longer if you want a room over the school holidays), and family rooms are harder to come across so it is worth booking early.

Sites such as www.airbnb.com have a huge range of properties to choose from, in particular many that are whole apartments – making self-catering possible.

Feed me

Breastfeeding is widely accepted across England and it is perfectly fine to feed in public. If you prefer privacy, most department stores, museums and galleries offer parent rooms with change facilities and feeding space.

Stay connected

The City of London's 'Square Mile' (the area that spans between Chancery Lane, Aldgate and down to the Thames) now has free Wi-Fi. If you are in the area, simply download the free app at www.thecloud.net/free-wifi/get-the-app. Most cafés, pubs, hotels and apartments also offer free Wi-Fi for patrons and guests.

Ticket deals

If you plan on visiting a number of attractions, it is well worth buying a multi-pass. There are a number on offer:

The London Pass: Including the Tower of London, Windsor Castle, Royal Observatory Greenwich, Tower Bridge Exhibition, Kensington Palace, the London Pass gives you entry to more than 60 popular attractions. It also gives you Fast Track entry into the more popular attractions, so you can jump those pesky queues. See www.londonpass.com for more details.

The RMG Big Ticket: Including the *Cutty Sark*, Royal Observatory and Peter Harrison Planetarium, you can see everything that Greenwich has to offer on one ticket. See www.rmg.co.uk/visit/tickets-and-prices for more details.

Merlin Combi Ticket: Including London Aquarium, London Dungeon, London Eye, Madame Tussauds, SEA LIFE – there are a number of different combinations available. All tickets also give you priority entrance to skip the queues. See www.visitsealife.com/london/ticket-prices for more details.

Index